FIRST IMPRESSIONS

DISCARD

First Impressions

FRESH LOOKS FOR ENTRYWAYS, HALLWAYS, AND FOYERS

ANNA KASABIAN

GLOUCESTER MASSACHUSETTS

ROCKPORT PUBLISHERS

First published in the United States of America by
Rockport Publishers, Inc.
33 Commercial Street
Gloucester, Massachusetts 01930-5089
Telephone: (978) 282-9590
Fax: (978) 283-2742
www.rockpub.com

Library of Congress Cataloging-in-Publication Data
Kasabian, Anna.
    First impressions : fresh looks for entryways, hallways,
and foyers / Anna Kasabian.
        p.   cm.
    ISBN 1-56496-861-8
    1. Entrance halls. 2. Corridors. 3. Interior decoration.
    I. Title.
    NK2117.E5 K38 2002
    747.7'9—dc21   2001005984

10 9 8 7 6 5 4 3 2 1

Design: Peter King & Company
Cover Image: © Wulf Brackrock/Jahreszeiten Verlag
Inside Back Flap Image: Tria Giovan
Photo Research: Wendy Missan
Project Manager: Ann Fox

Printed in China

To all the wonderful friends I have, friends who have opened their doors and shared their spirit with me.

Contents

FOREWORD

In addition to serving as the greeting area
for guests, an entryway is the main directional
artery of your home. Unless you have a
large home with lots of storage options, the
entryway is often earmarked as the place to
leave things. It is easy for entryways, hallways,
and foyers to become storage central
instead of an artistic or creative platform.

But with minimal planning and work, your
entryways can be beautiful, functional,
creative statements. As you think about
altering this space, I recommend you look
at your entryway as its own space first.
After all, you can always link this area to
the rest of your house by color or style—
that's easy. So think outside the box first!
Give yourself the chance to discover a
design path that brings something totally
new and exciting to this area of your home.

First analyze the space. Stand in your entry,
with the door open and behind you.
Examine the light. What kind of light does
this space receive? Is it warmed by morning
sun or is it filled with the dramatic light of
afternoon? Natural light colors different
areas in its own way and contributes to the
mood and design possibilities. For example,

if it's a north-facing room with little or no natural light, you may want to paint it a warm color and accent it in a way that suggests a warm hello. A big bench fronted with a colorful rug might accomplish just that. If you live in a city high-rise and have an entry with a wall of glass overlooking the architectural terrain below, you may decide to frame the drama in a high-gloss white paint.

Look at light sources in general—including windows, hall lights, lamps, and recessed light—and then see where color and texture merge nearby. The entryway could become a punctuation point of color, a peaceful work space, or a little oasis for art or glass collections.

Consider, too, the size of the space and the architectural qualities. If the entryway is big enough to function as a room, think about how you or a family member could use and enjoy it and still have it work perfectly as a place to greet guests. If it is really tiny or planted in the middle of merging halls, then maybe it's a place to make just one artistic statement.

A helpful way to further analyze and plan the space is to photograph it from different angles at different times of day. Take a few snapshots with the entryway directly in front of you, then get down on the floor and shoot up. Stand outside the door and shoot from the steps. Once you've developed the photos, line them up on a table for examination. This exercise will help you see the space in its own plane and in context.

The next step is thinking about your entryway's personal statement. *First Impressions* describes different styles that will help you develop your own entryway recipes. From casual to formal to your own style, you can pick and choose colors and mix and match floors, wall coverings, and accessories that, when put together, reflect your point of view.

INTRODUCTION

Think of all the homes you have known in your lifetime. Each has its own personality, distinct setting, and unique views day and night. Depending on the setting, the sun, moon, stars, and landscape come into view through the windows and doors quite differently.

And no matter which way you enter the property, whether you wind your way down a long driveway, weaving in and out of the greenery, or make your way up an old stone stoop in the city, your trip ends at the front door.

It's the first place that says hello to your guests and gives them a sense of you and your nest. Front doors are wonderful structures that let us pause and take in our surroundings before we ring the bell or clang the knocker announcing our arrival.

Some people take great care to decorate their front doors—in essence, they are the first personal statements about the inhabitants. Some people paint their doors bright colors, surround them in a bright palette of plantings, and then add accessories like an antique boot scraper or unique brass knocker. Others maintain a quiet and clean front door with one simple focal point. Study front doors through the ages—you will see that they are an art form that reflects a slice of the history of man and society.

In my travels, doors have taken me in and tapped my spirit. I have photographed them, walked up to them, and examined them as studies in life. And I am always left wondering what is behind that door. Is there more of the same or a total surprise?

Recently, on an antique hunting adventure, my husband found a little wooden music chair—with simple lines, childlike innocence, and a friendly posture—and we decided this would be the perfect engaging sculpture to have guests see as our front door opens. Situated above it is a photo of a fluffy cloud perched over the rounded edge of a bush. That visual, we thought, sums up what our home is about—a place that will make you smile, while offering the unexpected.

It was that design exercise that inspired me to write this book about entryways. Too often, this precious piece of real estate is simply designated for a table, a plant, and a pile of keys. Because these spaces are often ignored or decorated according to some obsolete conservative recipe, I felt a book on entryways was needed.

My goal is to give you visual tools and tips that will release your creativity and help you make the entryway of your home a punctuation point for who you are. Enjoy the views.

First
IMPRESSIONS

Entryways are the center of the home's traffic flow. In most houses, they are also the natural spot for piles of mail, newspapers, shoes, umbrellas, keys, and other assorted items. It is easy to lose the essential first impression of a beautiful home when entryways become more like storage areas.

The wonderful news about entryways, halls, and foyers is that a lot can be done with a little. These areas are easy to change—often with items on hand—and do not take a lot of time to transform into satisfyingly beautiful spaces. The first step is simple: Consider the entryway its own space or small room. By doing so, you may discover a design path that incorporates something totally new and exciting.

STARTING Fresh

USE WHAT YOU HAVE TO CREATE A NEW LOOK

ABOVE Sometimes, a single item is all that's needed to bring a foyer together. The graceful table shown here does just that and offers a space for showing off favorite collectibles. Notice how the simple chair presents a warm invitation, without clutter or intrusion into the traffic space.

A big decorating budget isn't necessary to give an entryway a fresh, new look. Most people probably already have several things—furnishings, lights, vases—that have pleasant qualities and characteristics that have been ignored because of poor placement. Isolating them and giving them a spotlight at the front door would give them new life.

If this strategy is appealing, begin by walking around your home and putting a tag on things you like that haven't been getting the attention they deserve. A desk, a lovely old lamp, or an antique clock that's been tucked into a dark corner for too long could fall into this category.

Once this exercise has been completed, go back to the front door and think about how to place any one or a few of those elements here. Think about the mood and personality you want to project to guests as they await your turn of the knob to welcome them inside. Decide if you want the entry to serve as an appetizer for the rest of your home's decor or if you want it to be a completely different statement, one that perhaps says more about how you want to make guests feel.

Do consider the entryway as a small room all its own. Furnish it with charming pieces that may be languishing elsewhere. Treat it as a gallery for a changing array of favorite vases, pictures, and pottery.

Do create unusual and surprising focal points: Paintings are nice, but what about hanging collections of antique porcelain plates? A grouping of three or more items works best to add color and dimension.

Do consider decorating walls with tiles—look at contemporary glass tile offerings as well as reclaimed, antique tile, depending on the mood you want.

Do consider scenic wallpapers or a tromp l'oeil painted panel to create atmosphere.

Do consider the classic, elegant look of contrasting floor tiles in different geometric patterns.

Do experiment. If you like floor tiles but prefer a less formal look, consider painting in big squares of color, or for polished drama, a single solid color in a high-gloss finish.

Don't get carried away with silk flowers—unless you can change them often, they'll become dirty and quickly lose their charm. Even a single fresh flower is a prettier, more soulful choice.

Don't let furnishings intrude even a little on the area for foot traffic—nothing is so attractive that you will want to detour around it many times a day.

TOP Serene and understated, the table and uphol-stered bench are timeless entryway classics. The best hall tables have a drawer to stow letters and keys. Keep the table handy to the bench but positioned so a seated guest has easy passage.

ABOVE Dressed and furnished in fabric and flowers, a foyer transformed into a wonderful cozy room makes a welcome view when the door swings open. Don't be afraid to group more than just a table so near the door; the charm of collections and a few well-upholstered pieces can be lovely.

OPPOSITE Here is an example of how simplicity can anchor a theme. Just a few embellishments make the point that this is all about country in the casual style.

ABOVE Our homes are our theaters, so to speak. With the right elements, we can recreate periods and turn back the clock!

Doorways

Walk down any street, and it will be evident how residents weave their identities into their yards, walkways, or stoops with their choices of plantings, fencing, and stone paths. Some yards are lush and rooted in color; others are more natural and allow greenery to grow without the mower or hedge-clipper's discipline. But it is the front door of each house that really describes a personality and offers a preview of a home's coming attractions.

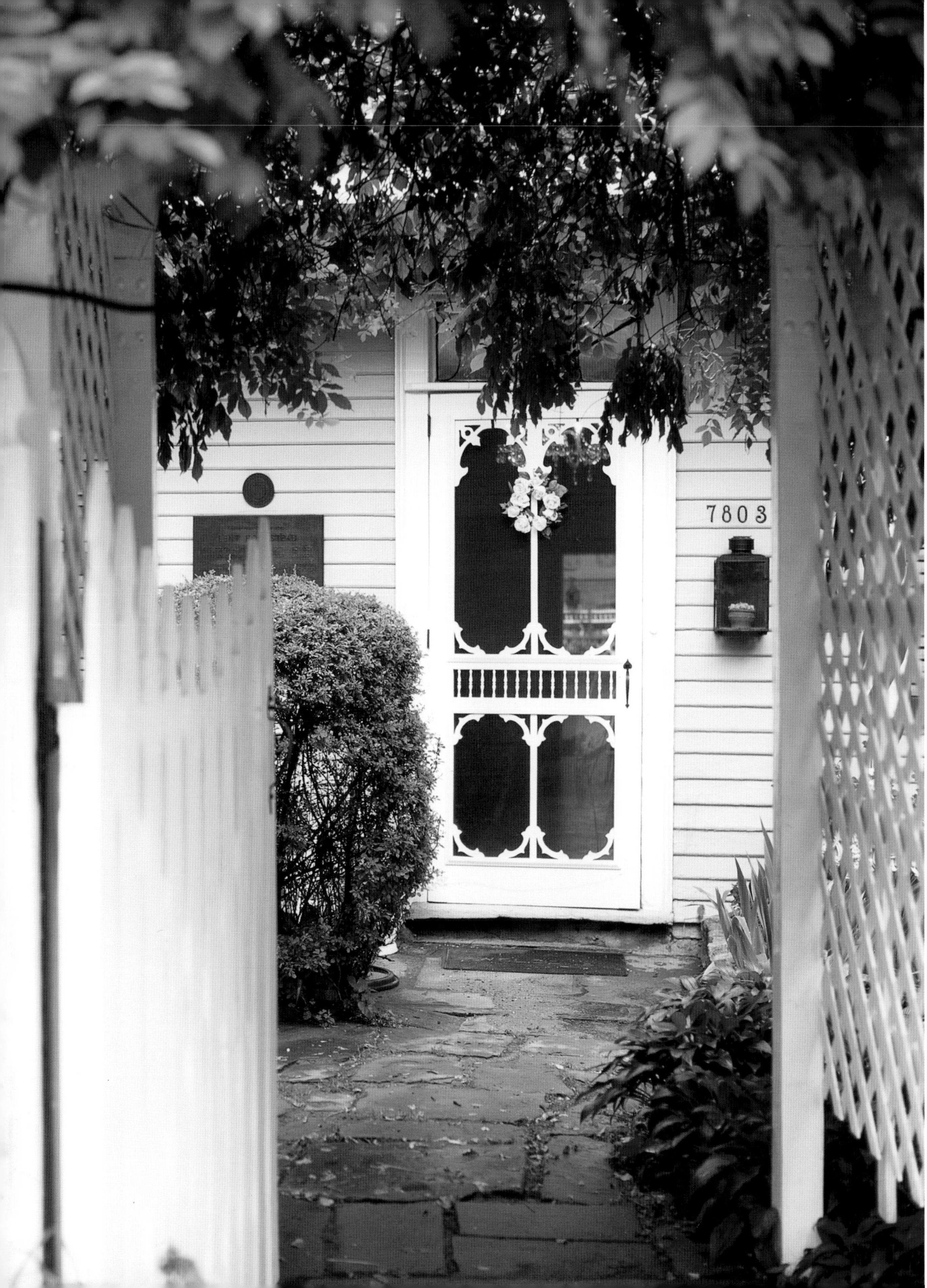
7803

Doorways offer many opportunities to say something special in a unique and creative way. Homeowners can take cues from the architectural style and setting of their homes and add elements to the front door that complement and highlight those details. On the other hand, by adding a design element that is more of a surprise and contrast, homeowners hint that they are full of surprises, too.

Doorways can also provide a personalized message about the home within. And, like the space just inside that open door, doorways offer the opportunity to provide a clear welcome and sometimes a quick peek at what's about to come.

The front door itself—whether it is antique wood or painted bright red—is the heart of the home. The door's accents—such as stone planters, an old, knotted wisteria plant, or a pine bench—work with the door to communicate a cohesive message.

Use your entryway to welcome, embrace, and make people smile. Spend some time making it right for you and them.

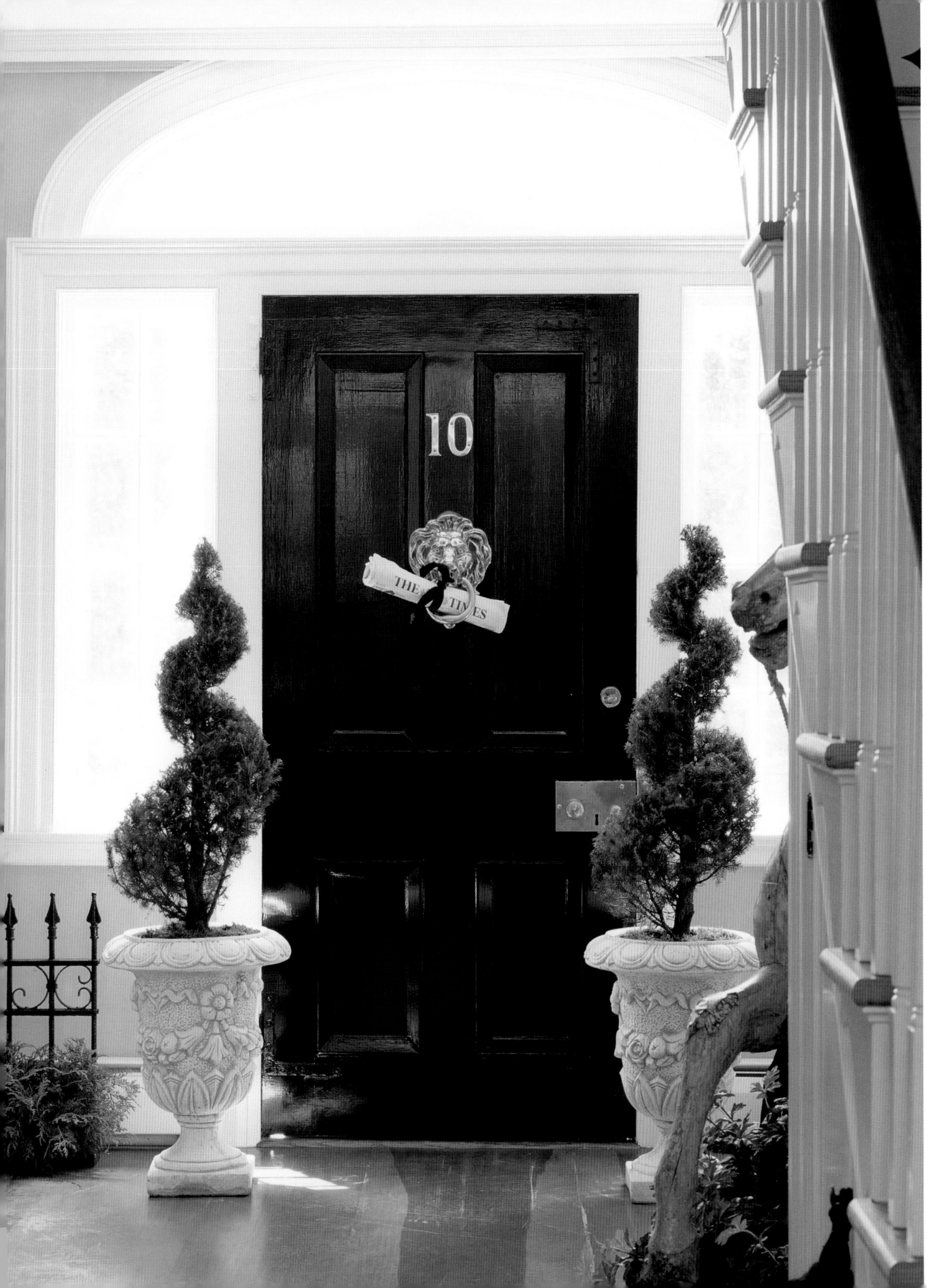
10
THE
TIMES

Here are some decorating ideas for your front door area:

- Think about replacing the front door entirely if it lacks character, is boring or featureless. Look into reclaimed doors. There are doors available that once were the doors to mansions, farmhouses, and even castles.

- If you'd like to create more interest in an already pretty door, consider adding an antique stained-glass panel or entire window, or investigate windows from periods you like and have a craftsman duplicate it.

- Investigate the possibilities of a glass outside door that has decorative ironwork on it.

- Think about painting your front door a color that contrasts with the exterior of your home. For example, if your house is red, consider painting the door black.

- Look into framing your front door with accents that complement the style of your home and property. Here are a few ideas to investigate: door knockers, from contemporary to antique and reproductions; doorbells; boot cleaners; lighting— over the door and on either side; and mailboxes.

- Don't ignore the value of plantings that will add color, texture, and dimension. Consider planters on either side of the door and climbing vines like wisteria that, with their twists and turns and rich bloom, will create a magical entry.

- If you have the artistic confidence and can work with a qualified craftsperson, consider changing the entire frame of your door. Some possibilities include framing the door in stone or even tile or creating a large border of glass and having your door be an unfinished, antique wood. If you explore tile, play with new ideas like using a thin ribbon multicolored tile that wraps the door.

- Integrate the pathway that leads to your door in the design scheme. Move away from the expected concrete sidewalk, and look at textures such as crushed shell, pebbles, and slate, for example. It's much more interesting to look at and the sound feedback is wonderful.

- Investigate planting shrubs or trees along the walkway to your door. Look into unexpected greenery solutions such as shrubs groomed into unusual shapes or tall Poplar trees that can create a corridor to your door.

- Consider planting flowers normally reserved for a cutting garden, and plant by the front door. For more fun, plant flowers that attract butterflies or certain bird varieties on the path.

- Don't forget to carry the lighting theme onto the pathway, too. Look at installing low lights along the path or sunken lights that just glow on the ground.

- Take advantage of seasons to add color, and change the view at your door with new plantings and wreaths.

CHAPTER 2

Stairways
AND STRUCTURE

LETTING THE ARCHITECTURE SPEAK

LEFT Here is an example of a stairway as the focal point. Notice how the dark wood stain on the steps and banister leads your eye up, up, and away, with a quick stop at the turn to look at an unusual piece of art.

STAIRWAYS AND Structure

LEFT Opting for a monotone stone keeps an entry-way open and calming. Notice, too, how this provides a backdrop for the rich, dark wood furnishings.

Consider installing risers and a banister that complement or contrast with the flooring at the base of the stairs. For example, if you have a black and white marble floor, installing a black wrought iron banister and painting wood risers black and white checks will bring your eye up, up, and away.

Warm up a cool entry by creating a rich color path with carpeting, or cool down an entry by choosing stone or marble for entry stairs and walls. Think about keeping the entryway theme but with a twist when it comes to wallpaper. If there are big florals in the entry, consider tiny ones here, and reverse the emphasis in the palette to keep it interesting. Or, keep visuals simple, and let the architecture speak for itself.

Do not forget the importance of lighting the path. Look into sconces that can climb the walls, and if the space is right, consider a dramatic chandelier centered over the staircase. The right lighting can accentuate the special architectural details of the staircase.

Finally, let a window on the staircase be a design asset. Consider installing custom-made stained-glass panels, or hunt the Internet or auctions for stained-glass windows that once lived in mansions or cottages. These will add color and enhance the views when light plays on your staircase.

THE STAIRCASE CAN BE A WONDERFUL PART OF YOUR ENTRY ROOMSCAPE, AND DEPENDING ON THE STAIRWAY STYLE—MODERN OR NOT—IT CAN ENHANCE AND ENRICH VIEWS.

How can the structure be linked to the entryway design? Use the wall space along the stairway—up to the very top—to display art that leads your guests upstairs. Situate the artwork on the wall so that it has rhythm, as opposed to a stagnant, repetitive look of square after square. For example, hang art so that each piece literally climbs the wall of the staircase at different levels. Also, consider positioning one large piece of art—such as a tapestry, oil, or photo collage—on a large, open wall after a dramatic turn in the stairway.

OPPOSITE Working with an imaginative architect can bring results like this entryway. The stunning stairway, reminiscent of the inside of a seashell, is the only sculpture this space needs.

ABOVE When designing an entryway with a new staircase, consider mixing open metal and wood flooring. The open stairs keep the entry open and crisp, and the wood warms up the space.

OPPOSITE An entry with a period staircase like this, as well as architectural detailing, can enhance a country theme. By painting the natural wood black with white detailing, the warm, country mood would swing into a cool, contemporary one.

CHAPTER 3

Hallways
AND FOYERS

NOT JUST PASSING THROUGH

LEFT When planning a space, don't forget about being practical. This back door leads to the yard and, perhaps, a garden, so it makes sense to have a stone or tile floor for easy sweeping and clean up. With all the natural light, filling in with potted plants makes sense, too; it also keeps the view inside as pretty as it is outside.

NOT JUST PASSING THROUGH
DO'S AND DON'TS:

Do bring in furnishings with a purpose.

Do consider displaying visual themes that align with personal or family activities.

Do consider armoires for storing everything from books to paints to tabletop easels.

Don't ignore the unique storage cubbies under the staircase.

Don't solve problems with expected solutions.

Don't forget to buy task lighting.

Don't treat this space like a showplace if it doubles as a workplace.

Don't forget a theme and palette can be continued up the stairs and on the banister.

Don't forget the decorative qualities of pillows and window seats.

Don't forget this floor space can be treated differently.

IN MOST HOMES, ENTRYWAYS FUNCTION AS MORE THAN A WELCOME AREA. WHERE THERE IS AVAILABLE SPACE, ENTRYWAYS MAY BE TREATED AND FURNISHED IN A WAY THAT MAKES THEM VERY SPECIAL LITTLE ROOMS. ALTHOUGH THEY ARE NOT ALWAYS THE MOST PRIVATE PLACE IN THE HOME, ENTRYWAYS, HALLWAYS, AND FOYERS CAN BE DESIGNED IN WAYS THAT ENCOURAGE FITTING ACTIVITIES. A DESK, FOR EXAMPLE, UNDER THE STAIRWELL COULD WORK WELL FOR WRITING OUT BILLS. A BENCH AND PIANO COULD BE PERFECT FOR MUSIC LESSONS AND PRACTICING.

Look at your layout to determine potential for a new use. Is there a big, winding staircase that has created an oasis of peace beneath? What can be placed there? A desk? A bookcase? A loveseat?

Many possibilities exist for the entryway. Picture the following unique themes with beloved furnishings, whether they are contemporary, antique, or a mixture. In addition, consider this a design zone where creative spirit can shine. Remember, the entryway design does not have to align with the rest of the house style; it can be its own art form.

LEFT When evaluating the design potential for an entryway, look first at the layout and existing structure before giving the room a designated purpose. Here, French doors make the entry its own little room. This homeowner chose to add a little table that can serve as a quiet place to read the morning paper and sort mail.

RIGHT With magnificent views to the open ocean, adding seating here makes sense. Guests or family members might just like to perch here for a while and take in the sounds, smell, and views of the ocean beyond. If your entry has special views like this, think about what can be added for guests and family to enjoy.

ESSENTIALS: UNIQUE
DESIGN POSSIBILITIES,
USE OF THEMED PALETTES,
STORAGE SOLUTIONS

NOT JUST PASSING
THROUGH TREASURES:
BIG, WINDING STAIRCASES;
ARMOIRES; WRITING DESKS;
WINDOW SEATS

NOT JUST PASSING
THROUGH DETAILS:
DECORATIVE PILLOWS,
TASK LIGHTING, STORAGE
CUBBIES, MUSICAL
INSTRUMENTS,
TABLETOP FOUNTAIN

NOT JUST Passing Through

A Place For Music

If space permits, the entry could be the perfect place to put a piano or a single chair for voice or music lessons. Keep musical instruments there, too, in full view. The piano is a perfect platform for a vase of fresh flowers or a pretty row or circle of little bud vases. Or consider it as a stand for a piece of sculpture that's been hidden away in a dark corner for too long. Go romantic, and place an antique candelabra on top, and light it regularly to enhance appreciation of this space. Fill the wall—floor to ceiling—with framed photos of children at recitals for a warm, engaging theme.

Purchase an interesting storage piece for music books. For example, an old jeweler's display case could serve as a bookcase or music books could be stacked inside a tall, thin bookcase just wide enough for the books. When it's time to hear a new piece of work, gather guests and family members there and keep stackable folding chairs under the stairs for an impromptu concert.

Finally, think about ways to develop the area's theme. For example, painting the floor a solid cream background, and having a faux painter add a few musical notes to the floor—not too many and in either a variety of color or one, like gold—may be the perfect touch. Add a note or two to the window sill, if there is one in this area. Adding antique, framed music sheets in old or new, clean-lined frames is another entryway art option.

RIGHT Here, a beautiful harp serves as the focal point of a long hallway. The patterned wood floor creates a pathway to the harp.

Let the Games Begin

The entry and foyer could act as a game room in a home where the family room is too small or the television is too noisy for board game concentration. Consider adding a drop-leaf table, a few chairs, and a wooden chest filled with board and card games to the area. Or, if there's room, purchase a bench with game storage underneath. And, finally, another option would be to construct a window seat with storage underneath, and keep the drop leaf table to the side. Try painting a checker board on the floor beneath the table and chairs for more fun. If the wall space allows, wallpaper this area differently than the rest of the main hall. For example, using a wallpaper that resembles suede or a library-wall print will enhance the game or club look.

LEFT Even if entryway space is small, the right furnishings can make it a place to linger. Here, an entry off the garden provides an excellent space for tea, the crossword puzzle, or a board game for two. Notice how the tile floor extends outdoors and how tucking the furniture against the wall keeps traffic moving. Take advantage of entry qualities like these —nice light, windows, views—and turn it into a room with a dual purpose.

A Special Reading & Writing Zone

Is there space to tuck a comfy chair and reading lamp under a stairwell or at the base of the foyer? Consider making this a place where you only read certain topics, and keep a small bookshelf nearby for only those topics. For example, if the dining room is the next room over, perhaps this would be a nice place to retreat to plan party menus and choose wines. Keep reference books nearby with a favorite pen and a special pad of paper. With a phone close by, calling in catering and wine orders is easy. Or, keep that leather-bound journal tucked on a nearby shelf, and make this a writing hideaway when the house is quiet.

Decorative accents could include glass jars filled with wine corks, framed wine bottle labels, a collection of antique bottle openers, pen-and-ink drawings of set tables and china, or a wall filled with miniature oil paintings that focus on grapes and vineyards or black-and-white photographs of parties or wine making.

LEFT Here is the perfect set-up for writing or reading. Big, comfy pillows perched atop a built-in bench warm up what could be a stark, cool corner.

A Place to Draw

Perhaps the entry has the space for a tabletop or full-sized easel. Bring in a side table with a drawer to store art supplies, a stool (topped with wood or covered in fabric), and a table or floor lamp with a bulb that mimics natural light. If it's preferable to hide the drawing materials, then use a tabletop easel that folds up and can be stored in the table drawer. For paints, inks, or drawing pencils, use a simple Shaker wood box, an antique paint box, or an attractive cigar box. Another option is to find an armoire and have a carpenter build shelving inside for art supplies. A small art stool could be tucked in the bottom of the armoire, so the armoire remains the entry's focal point.

RIGHT If this bench seat doubles as storage, you can keep drawing materials hidden away.

OPPOSITE The space under or at the base of stairs can provide a wonderful hideaway for both adults and children. With proper lighting and storage, it becomes a cozy area for sketching or reading. Notice the thoughtfully placed shelving next to the window seat here. It's perfect for storing art supplies and books, or it could just as easily be used as a place to serve cocktails.

Special Containers for Special Collections

An entry can easily become a showcase for collectibles. For a contemporary feel, construct glass shelving from floor to ceiling or use reclaimed barn wood for the country look. Purchase a glass-fronted cupboard or use the tops of other furnishings—such as chests, armoires, and tables—as bases for collectibles. A locking armoire, chest (one that can't be taken out the door!), or antique steamer trunk is also a good place to keep receipts and records of your possessions. For decorative accents, stay with the collectible theme and find complementary framed art, fabrics, and wall coverings. For example, if you wanted to devote this space to a collection of tabletop sailing ships, take the boat theme and bring it to the walls with brass lanterns, blue wallpaper with gold stars, and fabrics with sea-themed patterns. In addition, an old steamer trunk and an antique captain's desk would also add to the space.

RIGHT Think about creating an interesting corner to display antique furnishings, art, and rare books. Decide on a theme—such as boats—to pull it all together.

OPPOSITE A lack of a separate library doesn't have to be a problem. Consider creating a small reading area in the entry as these homeowners did. These glass-walled bookshelves work perfectly in this long hall, and the twin leather chairs at the front door are both practical and inviting.

A Garden Nook

For the gardener without storage space, the entry can be transformed into a garden storage center for everything from seeds to pots to hand shovels. With the right furnishings, the foyer can be styled casually, but remain pristine and pretty. Imagine using a wonderful old marble-topped bureau for this purpose. The drawers can hold bulky items, and the marble top can be used to hold pretty pots. Seed packets and soil can be hidden inside brightly colored, hand-painted pottery jars. Keep the area in bloom year round by having a faux painter create a garden scene that wraps the walls in the space or covers a wall screen. Painting the screen a plain color and decoupaging old postcards of gardens to the sides is also an option. Or instead of a painted screen, cover the screen in fabric that has a garden theme, and sew pockets to hold the seeds, scissors, and other accessories.

ABOVE With a bit of added storage, this gardener's nook serves double-duty: as a practical place to store tools and as a dreamy sanctuary.

OPPOSITE Proper task lighting and nearby shelving make it easy to get to work in this charming spot.

A Home Workstation

With just enough space for a writing table, an entry can be a place for specific tasks like shopping by phone or paying the bills. Purchase furnishings that can adequately store catalogs and hold a checkbook, bills, stationery, and stamps. Because most homes have mailboxes situated at the front door, it's the perfect place to keep up with bills and paperwork. Station a mail outbox here, too, so you will always remember to take out the mail. Look at a secretary-style desk, a tambour desk with shelves, a writing surface, and drawers when outfitting the entryway space.

The Right Place for Spirits

For those with limited space in their dining rooms, the entry can be the perfect storage area for wine and spirits, as well as glassware. And, if space allows, a mini-bar can be placed here with a few chairs so when guests arrive, they can get their drinks before entering the formal dining or living room areas. If plumbing is nearby, consider installing a wet bar and closing off the area with a screen. As suggested earlier, the screen could be painted, covered in fabric, or collaged with photos. In this scenario, a collage of old wine bottle labels or photo prints of bars—in hotels, neighborhoods, boats, and trains—may be appropriate. When purchasing furnishings for storing bottles, consider the Bonnetiere armoire, which is tall and thin.

LEFT In a spacious entry, large pieces of furniture —ones that are nice to look at and serve a purpose— can be introduced. Here, a wonderful old clock chimes the guests in and a country buffet stores collectible dishes and other less frequently used dining supplies. Without cluttering the space, the large pieces help guests appreciate the home's beautiful wood floors and classic architectural details. Everything else in here, from the stack of colorful Shaker boxes to the chair, add to the country theme.

A Place to Meditate

If foot traffic through the entryway is minimal, it might be a very quiet, pleasant place to meditate. Think about putting a grass cloth rug in the space, as well as a few pillows covered in natural fibers in subdued colors. Or go with patterns that depict reeds or leaves to keep the calm. In this same space, you can also create a *tokonoma*, a place where one special piece of Asian art is displayed—it could be as simple as a tiny teacup or handmade bowl that perches on a small table or ledge. Add a colorful backdrop with an Asian-made fabric scroll. If there is a small window under the stairwell, think about installing a noren instead of a curtain. A noren is a linen, hand-painted piece of fabric that hangs in windows and doorways. For natural inspiration, get some narrow terra-cotta boxes and plant grass. Sit these on the window sills or on the floor, if there is lots of sunlight. Another nice addition would be a tabletop water sculpture; the sound of water running over pebbles is very soothing. Finally, investigate whether the environment is right for bonsai or potted bamboo.

LEFT If your entry needs to maintain the theme of the rest of the house but is a good spot to meditate, just keep the area simple and calming.

ABOVE Here is a wonderful example of how a different version of a palette can make an entry feel totally inviting! This window seat, piled with pillows and offering a drape closure, is the ultimate in cozy. Think about whether there's room to construct this in an entry space, and pay attention to design details like the molding in front of the curtains; they can add to the interest level. This would also be a nice place to read or meditate.

OPPOSITE Benches, chairs, and chests of drawers can all work to make an entry more useful. A sunny entry is the ideal spot for needlepoint, knitting, or card writing, so keep your supplies handy. And don't forget a nice reading or task light.

MAINTAINING STYLE WITH ENTRYWAY LIGHTING

Entryway lighting needs to be bright enough to light the way for evening guests, but not so bright that they feel they have entered a public building. With all the choices in lighting available today, lighting can become an integral part of the design scheme, regardless of your style.

In order to properly plan where lights will go or where they are needed, diagram all major furnishings on paper. The areas that need direct light and the areas that only require decorative and accent lighting will be evident.

Before purchasing lighting, take note of your entryway ceiling height, and look at the size of the entryway space. If it's big as well as high, choose a major light fixture that will fit the space proportionately. A light that is too small for the space will not provide the necessary light distribution. Add decorative or accent lighting that complements the design and mood of the area. For example, if you install an antique crystal and brass chandelier, consider adding wall sconces that have crystal or brass accents. If collecting lamps and lighting is a hobby, the entryway is the perfect place to show off a collection while maintaining an eclectic style.

When considering secondary decorative lighting, don't forget candlelight. It's perfect for evening entertaining and can be placed on wall space among regular lights. Also, consider an all-candle chandelier. Varying the bulb wattage so each light serves a specific design or function is another way to accent the mood of the entryway.

Finally, take time to look at the universe of lighting before making a selection. Visit at least two showrooms, look through magazines (not only display ads but the classifieds, which often have unusual items), and surf the Internet before you make your final choices.

OPPOSITE In a large, two-story foyer like this, consider simple up-lighting and recessed lighting that does not steal the show.

CHAPTER 4

Casual
STYLE

LEFT In a small entry, you can still make a significant statement that welcomes guests. Just keep it simple, like this. The little pine table serves up a pretty, fresh flower arrangement and directs the eye to the old stone wall decorated with antiques based on a single theme. The casual slate floor works perfectly since the garden is just outside the door.

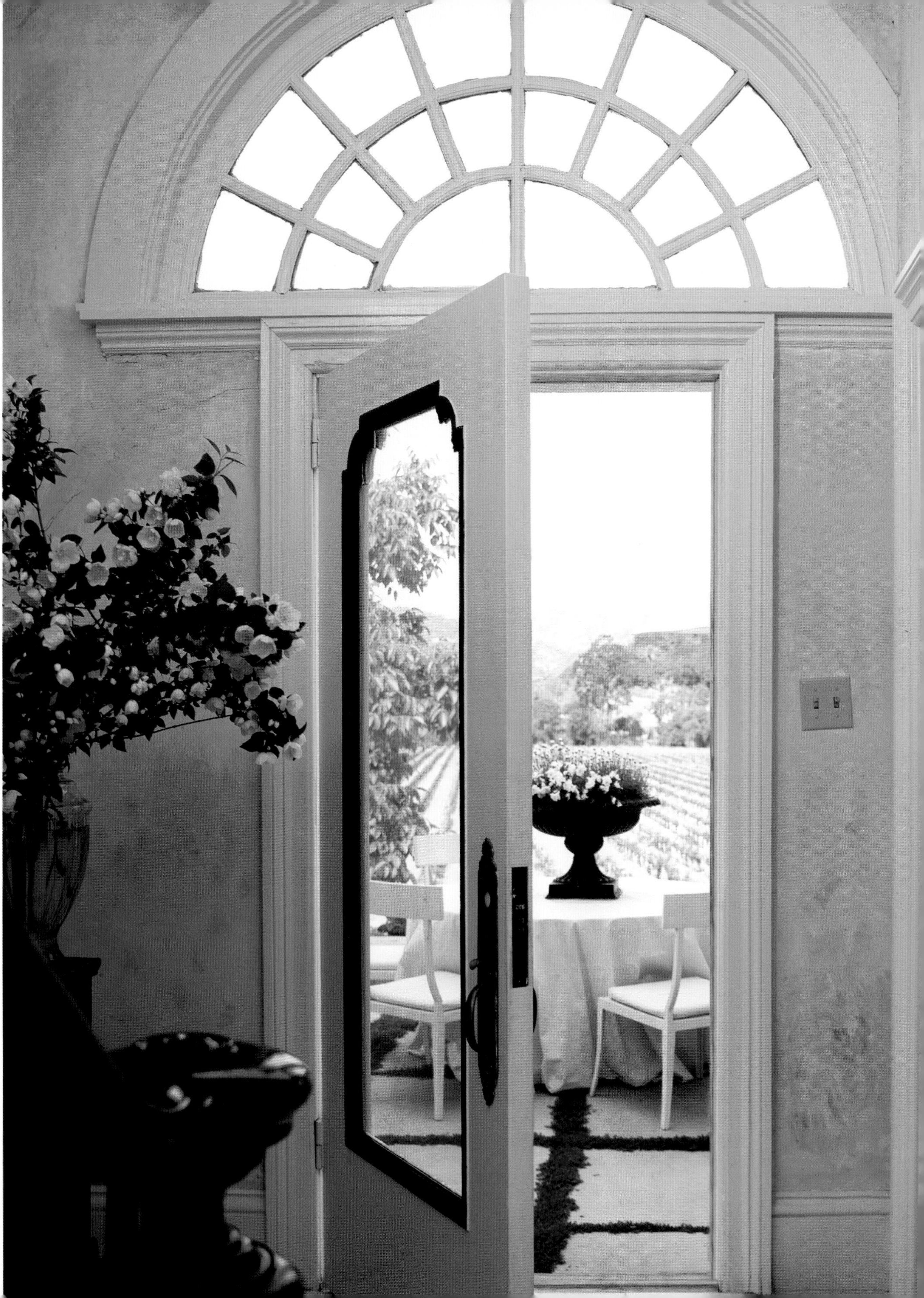

THERE ARE MANY WAYS TO CREATE A CASUAL-STYLE ENTRYWAY AND STILL HOLD ON TO A VERY DISTINCTIVE LOOK. IT JUST TAKES THE RIGHT MIX OF FURNISHINGS, FABRIC, FLOORING, AND COLOR. CASUAL STYLING ENCOURAGES A MIXING AND MATCHING ON ALL DESIGN LEVELS.

Casual style suggests an easygoing design route that is comfortable, both physically and visually. It has everything to do with being engaging. Casual style is easy and pleasant to be around and can also be whimsical. Unlike some formal spaces that say "don't touch" or scream "fragile," casual says, "touch me," "sit on me."

A casual entry can, in fact, be a mix of authentic antique country furnishings, contemporary, cottage style, and flea-market finds—or it can be composed of just one style. It's up to you. The most important thing for you to do is determine the shapes, colors, and textures that please you, suggest informality, and work in the space.

The following examples of casual mixes also incorporate some elements of visual surprise:

• Mixing together country, contemporary, and flea-market furnishings creates a casual style that welcomes guests into the entryway. Consider a major piece of furniture such as a desk made from an old barn door. If your walls are bead-board and the room a bit dark, introduce a contemporary rug with a pattern of squares that consists of big blocks of color—red, blue, yellow, and green—and sit the desk atop that. Next, fill the wall behind the desk with flea-market finds, such as old magazine advertisements framed in contemporary glass frames with no wood edging. Hang the frames from wood molding added to the walls, dropping them from wire.

• Paint adds a bright, cheerful feeling to a casual entry filled with a mix of old and new. Imagine your major piece of furniture is an old piano. It may be fairly beat up but it sounds wonderful. Make this a piece of art by painting it bright red all over, except for the legs, which are painted white. Painting the floor white and adding musical notes in black that surround the piano legs adds a whimsical feeling. On the wall behind the piano, frame photos of famous musicians from the pages of old books. The frames should be a mix of old and new.

OPPOSITE With a view as spectacular as this, add an outdoorsy look to an entryway to draw a visual line to the outdoors.

Makeover Advice

FOR CASUAL-STYLE ENTRYWAYS

One of the first things to do before venturing out on a shopping spree is to empty the entryway and look at the clean space. The goal with any style of entryway is to accentuate the area's best attributes and, ultimately, lead people into the home. Grand or tiny, the entryway also cues guests to the left, right, or straight ahead.

When the space is empty, make note of elements like:

- Natural light and opportunities to add light
- Floor space and materials
- Architectural attributes
- Wall space and attributes

To make the design process enjoyable, prepare for the adventure and expose yourself to lots of design possibilities. If you want to create a casual entry that has lots of country elements, visit local historic homes and inns to see furnishings, palettes, collections, and flooring in their purest form. Those experiences will help you

LEFT Add a casual style to your entry by mixing a few special antique treasures with an assortment of old framed art. The natural light and neutral walls and floors place special attention on the collections. Use staircase windows and landings to guide guest upstairs by adding pretty plants and pots.

decide whether to go French country or English, or whether collecting Depression-era glassware or bentwood boxes is more appealing. Eventually, the design components of one or more eras will appeal and serve as a starting point for entryway decoration. If it is preferable, in the end, you can create a casual design stew by mixing and merging periods.

Do the same design homework no matter what style you like. Go to flea markets and contemporary crafts fairs, purchase magazines from abroad, and study unfamiliar palettes and trends. The more you expose yourself to, the more interesting the possibilities that will surface.

Use the Internet to explore a range of design possibilities for fabrics, furnishings, flooring, and lighting. Try plugging in general search phrases such as "furniture," "cottage style," "painted furniture," "country furniture," or the names of specific design elements, such as "English country furniture."

Consider maintaining a notebook of rooms, palettes, and furnishings you like. Jot down favorites, as they will likely end up on a shopping list, and develop a budget! You can do this with any style you are interested in gathering information on.

Once those preliminary activities have been completed, it's time to get to work on examining some ideas that can make your entryway just perfect for you and your family—starting with how to create a casual entryway.

CASUAL-STYLE ENTRYWAYS DO'S AND DON'TS:

Do take a look at the entry when it's empty to plan the new look.

Do accentuate the architectural attributes of the space.

Do visit historic homes and inns as well as contemporary hotels for inspiration.

Do subscribe to auction house catalogs to learn about different furniture styles and art.

Do consider tile as an option for casual entry walls.

Do consider different painting techniques for floors and walls, including stenciling and sponging.

Do investigate wallpaper mural options and faux painting techniques that bring the outside view inside.

Do surf the Internet to see new products and old.

Do consider accenting with collectibles.

Do create a scrapbook of items you see that you love; this will help you plan future purchases for your entry.

Do consider painting wood floors.

Don't be in a hurry to finish this room. Take the necessary time.

Don't use artificial flowers. Use live ones instead.

Don't be afraid to mix different styles.

Don't ignore unusual pieces that may take on new life in your entry.

Don't forget about reclaimed woods, stone surfaces, and architectural details.

Don't depend on one kind of light source, and think of lighting as an accent to your design theme.

Don't forget about milk paint as an option.

Don't go to your first auction with the idea of buying. Go to listen and learn.

Don't forget that real plants can add color, dimension, and texture.

ESSENTIALS: FABRICS THAT
ARE COMFORTABLE AND NO
FUSS; FURNISHINGS THAT
INVITE YOU TO USE THEM

CASUAL TREASURES: SHAKER
DRYSINK AND WASHSTAND,
TAVERN TABLE, SHAKER
BOXES, HAND-BLOWN GLASS
VASES, GLASS SHELVING,
SCULPTURES, STEAMER
TRUNK, OLD POSTCARDS

CASUAL DETAILS: PAINTED
FURNITURE, POTTERY (OLD
AND NEW), HOOKED RUGS

CASUAL MIXES: PINE
BENCHES, PAINTED FLEA
MARKET FURNISHINGS WITH
BOLD COLORS AND PAT-
TERNS, WHIMSICAL PRE-
PAINTED FURNITURE OR
ACCENT PIECES, ENTRY FLOOR
PAINTED WITH HIGH GLOSS
PAINT OR WITH FLOOR ART

Casual Entryway Furnishings: The Range

A casual-style entryway can include authentic antiques, country, contemporary, and flea market furnishings. Try mixing two or more styles together. Think in terms of some pieces as being functional, like a desk or armoire to store glasses, and others as decorative accent pieces that anchor or emphasize a theme.

CASUAL ANTIQUE AND COUNTRY FURNISHINGS

Study eighteenth- and nineteenth-century offerings with clean, simple designs. To research the look and cost of authentic pieces, respected auction houses or antique dealers often offer catalogs of items for purchase in the period of interest. Authentic country furnishings range in tones from blonde pines to deep, dark cherry.

If you want to merge contemporary furnishings with country and maintain some visual continuity, look at Shaker-style furnishings that typically have straight, crisp lines and gentle curves.

As you develop your casual entryway, think about themes and repetition of those themes in different ways. For example, consider a New England server. This piece can be an attractive focal point with practical uses as

well. Its drawers could be used for storing infrequently used linen napkins, candles, and candleholders. If you need it as a server during the holidays, simply roll it into the room. And while this piece can lean towards a formal look, you can control the casual intensity in other design elements including rugs, window fabric, wall art, wall color, wallpaper, and even lamps. Hand-hooked and needlepoint rugs—for example, in country-style patterns—can themselves turn up the volume on casual. But so can a contemporary whimsical rug that depicts childlike color blocks and is finished with uneven edges that themselves form islands of art.

Suppose you find a wonderful old New England server that fits your space perfectly. How can you build around that piece with a theme? Think about the obvious theme of entertainment. Here are some possibilities:

- Line the walls with a framed collection of new or old place cards or invitations, and seed the wall collage with your favorite photos of family events.

- Have a faux painter create a country scene on the floor or wall and have all objects—trees, fences, pond, etc.— created by stringing words together, such as: *datetimeplacepleasejoinusforaparty*

Themes, or a repetition of themes, help

to pull the casual entryway look together. Imagine placing a courting bench in your entryway—the bench has two seats on a curve, each facing opposite directions and sharing an armrest. This unusual piece could become a conversation piece as well as a functional object. The seats could be used as the base for two antique iron garden urns, each holding twin topiaries, to create an engaging, welcoming view.

This wonderful piece could inspire a communications theme. Accents for this theme could include:

- a shelf lined with old telephones

- an antique telephone booth

- an art collage made with all the cards saved over the years including holiday cards, graduations, wedding, birth announcements, and even love letters! Think about what you have tucked away in boxes or in scrap books that you just never have the time to look at.

- a big, colorful poster that depicts people talking on the phone

To keep the look a mix of casual country and modern, introduce contemporary accents like lamps with glass shades, or big billowy curtains with thick, bold colored stripes.

The simple lines of a Danish country washstand accented with a marble top, a pantry closet, or a Swedish jelly cupboard are also good entryway possibilities, and each offers different accenting opportunities. These big wood structures add warmth to the space and provide a great base for design elements mentioned earlier. To develop themes that align with your antique country piece, look at the original function of the piece and see how you can branch off.

To further incorporate antique and country furnishings in the casual style, the Shaker Sabbath day dry sink—the original design dates back to the 1700s—with three little pegs, a shelf, and under-cupboard storage, could make the perfect casual entryway addition. The pegs can hold keys, for example; the shelf can hold the daily mail; and the cupboard could store mittens and scarves.

Here are some casual-style decorating ideas for the entry that use this dry sink, or a similar piece, as a focal point. These examples use a mix of country and other styles that provide a welcoming, casual feel to the entryway:

- To continue the country theme, line the floor on either side of the sink with a tight row of terra cotta pots, all shapes and sizes, and plant them with grass.

Paint the wall behind the sink a buttery shade of yellow and accent moldings with tangerine. Stagger wood shelving up and down the wall behind the sink. Sponge the shelving in brighter tones of yellow, tangerine, and a mix of the two, and introduce a collection of old framed garden magazine covers. Put down a multi-colored braided rug or runner with a darker version of your wall palette.

- To create a mix of country and contemporary: Line the floor with a collection of blown glass pots of contrasting sizes, shapes and colors—from tall and thin to big and round. Fill them with dried hydrangea, and vary the colors, lavender to white, pot to pot. Paint the wall behind the sink brick red and accent moldings in lavender. Add glass shelving to the wall; create a straight line but vary the shelf lengths. Put a collection of contemporary and flea market-find clocks on the shelves.

Other visually interesting pieces to consider—each with varied modern-day uses—include a Shaker washstand, a wall cupboard with a drop-down surface that acts as a desk, and a sewing desk with four drawers for storage. Depending on their size and your entry, you could introduce one of these or more.

Another interesting option is the antique Pennsylvania tavern table that can be found in a wood blend of painted maple with a pine base and tiger maple top. This can serve as a base for a collection of old glass or serve as a practical table to hold mail. Shaker boxes could also be used for this purpose; one for new mail and one for what needs to be mailed.

Or, there's the slant-front country desk that you can find in a rich wood combination of black walnut, cherry, and curly maple, complete with a cupboard on the lower half. This could turn out to be a great place to do bills, a task you may like to keep out of your study. Having an authentic antique like this in the entry, especially one with lots of elements to view, is a worthy showpiece that can be subtly adorned with, for example, an old hand-blown glass vase brimming with wildflowers.

Straight-lined, simple, narrow benches are also a good choice for casual entryways and can be used in addition to the furnishings mentioned above. There are many styles— from Danish country pine to the classic Windsor settee—that are good entryway choices.

OPPOSITE Warm wood tones, yellow, black, and white — what could be more casual or welcoming? When thinking about the design components of an entry, gather things in your home that you truly love and that may have not gotten proper attention in other rooms. Bring them to the entryways and see if their special qualities surface. Here, a wonderful mix of antique pieces thrive in this light, airy space. The stenciled stairway also says welcome—come on up.

CASUAL CONTEMPORARY FURNISHINGS

To create a casual contemporary entry, explore the world of painted furniture. Some manufacturers today are keeping the lines on tables sleek, offering tabletops in natural wood and trimming the table base or legs with lots of bold color and patterning. Look on the Internet for manufacturers that use a bright palette and whimsical painted patterns to really see a broad range. In addition, think about mixing one oddly-colored piece into the grouping.

Other manufacturers are reproducing antique-styled chairs with classic lines and painting them with a distressed look. A popular theme is white on white with gold accents. Others are reproducing bucolic country scenes and garden motifs on armoires, for example, and aging them through special painting techniques.

Another area to explore is whimsical, sculpted furniture. There are little loveseats that are shaped like keyboards and chairs shaped like a high heel shoe.

Explore glass options in tables, benches, and vases. Look first at what is offered by craftsmen and artists; although their pieces may cost a little more, this craftsmanship will bring a more interesting look to your entry. In general, it's advisable to put fewer elements in your entry that are more visually interesting rather than many items that have nothing new to say to you or your visitors. To get ideas go online, or plan some trips to local crafts fairs.

Study carpet offerings as well. There are wonderful contemporary rug designs out there that look like contemporary wall art. Depending on what you find, they can take the lead for your contemporary entryway's palette.

Certainly the easiest and least expensive way to make a contemporary design statement here is to wrap the entire entry—from the floor to the walls to the ceiling—in a hip color scheme. Imagine high gloss white floors, yellow walls, and a raspberry ceiling. Tuck the shoe-shaped chair in a corner, create a zigzag pattern of shelving where you perch a collection of multi-colored glass mugs, and you are getting onto a very exciting design path.

FLEA-MARKET FINDS

Finally, consider flea market finds to round out the look of your casual entry. Use flea market finds as accent pieces or, if you find large pieces like old trunks or nicely shaped chairs, you can have fun painting and refurbishing them.

Here are some design ideas with flea market finds:

- Maintain the casual contemporary look by painting the trunk or chair snow white, or go down the whimsy road and paint boldly colored patterns on the pieces.

- Mix and match what you do with a trio of pieces—such as a chest, a flat-topped table, and a chair—and create a little arrangement for your entryway.

- Introduce dramatic color by hanging or lining up colorful pottery or a collection of odd china in several different patterns. Have some fun and go with the theme of tacky. Paint your shelving different colors and use doilies or linens as well.

- Fill the wall in your entry with old walking sticks. Take the theme further and introduce old postcards themed on hiking and climbing.

- Take that old steamer trunk and either line it with an antique floral-patterned wallpaper, a polka dot pattern, or paint it your favorite color. Create a platform, swing it open, and fill the ledge with a collection of candlesticks and candles—all colors, all sizes, new and old.

- Go with a music theme and collect a bunch of old record players. Have the oldest as the centerpiece on a table (paint it bright red), and display the rest as you please in the space. Frame old music sheets, playbills, or concert hall maps for the walls, and take the theme to the floor by painting black and white stripes that mimic a keyboard.

LEFT AND ABOVE When you design an entry-
way, think in terms of "less is more." Notice how that
concept is at work here, and how the owners have
created a crisp, clean, welcoming space.

Casual Foyer Floors

PAINTING FOYER FLOORS WITH A MODERN FLAIR

If you like the cool, crispness of an all-white theme, paint a foyer floor white, giving all-white furnishings the look of beautiful ice sculptures. Use a high-gloss paint, and a very unique look is created, especially if your floors have wide planks. Consider this approach a great cover-up for floors that are structurally sound, but have a few sins of time.

Other floor painting themes to think about include:

- Create large contrasting squares of color—from black and white to yellow and brown or green and black.
- Emphasize the beauty of old, wide floor-boards by drawing the eye down to colorful hand-drawn designs like diamond shapes, stripes, or even triangles in different colors. Or say something special on your floor by stenciling a poem or the family tree.
- Go artsy and let the foyer floor be an art canvas. Experiment on paper first, or copy your favorite piece of modern art on the floor using an art projector that will project the shape on the floor. Then paint away.
- Experiment on plywood with combing paint for a whimsical approach. Imagine a black floor combed with lime green, and topped with that little trio of white furnishings.
- Look through magazines to find a contemporary rug pattern that you love, and turn that into a painted floor pattern. Paint it in front of the furniture in the entryway, and draw guests into the space.
- Consider adding color, dimension, and texture by painting the stairs with a simple countrified pattern if the entryway has a staircase. Get inspiration for shapes and colors by looking at quilts and hand-hooked rugs, but keep it clean to embrace the modern look.

KEEPING WOOD FLOORS AU NATUREL

If you plan to redo an entryway floor, installing new or reclaimed wood can provide a warm welcome mat for guests, while upholding the purity of the clean and modern look.

Before deciding on wood—white pine, maple, ash, or cherry—look at all the possibilities. Each wood varies in tone, surface, and width, so it's especially helpful to visit a wood flooring store. Seeing the many wood varieties in addition to the detailing possibilities will inspire you. Most wood flooring stores also have floor samples that show off wood patterns and borders in complementary tones. You could easily discover that a geometric wood pattern on the floor mimics a round rug and keeps the look clean, modern, and warm.

For a more casual look, think about wide planks, such as pine or old recycled barn boards for the ultimate rustic look. For a modern casual look, consider bleaching and pickling woods so they lighten and brighten a room and give darker furnishings an interesting platform upon which to perch.

Or consider mixing the entryway with some more rustic stones or tiles. Look at the selections of manufacturers that offer unusual limestone and slate. There are also international companies that recycle stone entryways and floors from castles and churches, which could create a most interesting entryway accent. Refer to books

that depict old ways of patterning stone and mixing colors.

As for reclaimed wood, many businesses sell wood floors they have saved from old homes, churches, factories, and barns. Reclaimed flooring can—with its worn planks and patterns—enrich an entryway and provide a beautiful, warm base for furnishings. When using reclaimed flooring, ask about nail detailing and using nails that are modern versions of the handmade nails.

Bring the garden theme inside by adding a pretty wrought iron bench and some potted plants by a painted wall. Look for storage solutions that add color.

INCORPORATING STONE, TILE, AND MOSAIC

Don't let painted or natural hardwood floors stop you from integrating hard surfaces like tile or stone into your entryway. Devote a portion of the floor area to stone, tile, or mosaic to create a small pattern, or cover a small portion of the entryway with a stone that complements your palette and enriches and diversifies the view.

Good choices to maintain a more modern, casual style at floor level would be clean, smooth, and shiny surfaces. Consider big blocks of white ceramic tile buttoned with small squares of color—from bright red to midnight blue and black. Investigate the new glass tiles that come in solid colors.

Look at creating unusual patterns of color with oddly shaped and inconsistently sized tiles that come together. For example, mix big squares with small ones and create a border with rectangles. Use a contemporary palette that also suggests casual, like burnt orange (smallest squares), robin's egg blue (big tiles), and rectangles of beige to link and border. Or, create borders and links with thin rectangles—two blue, two orange, two yellow in a repeating pattern, and move from there to a little larger border of solid color and keep the central part of the floor one color.

Think about creating a tile rug that leads guests into your foyer and home. Keep it simple with a solid color mosaic rug that's

3 feet wide (1 m), and wrap it in two different colors, two tiles deep. For a clean, contemporary, neutral palette, look into French limestone; the champagne hue and texture provide a quiet backdrop for warm wood furnishings. Picture a simple pine bench perched atop the limestone and, for color, a row of copper watering cans alongside filled with fresh red tulips.

Be creative and design an ultramodern art piece on the floor with mosaics or tile. In the right foyer this could be the centerpiece and palette leader for the area. It could be as simple as three reeds of tall grass in a sea of sand-colored mosaics. Keep the nature theme, and bring in various interesting, low wood containers brimming with real grass, and stretch them across a narrow wood or metal table.

Lighting Casual Hallways

ABOVE In this long, narrow entry, different-shaped furnishings create an interesting and welcoming place. And don't forget the importance of lighting to give guests something to look at and enjoy. In this entry, the twin leopard-spotted shades contrast nicely with the overhead candlelight fixture. The latter is a nice touch when there's a special occasion.

Entryway lighting should be decorative and functional. The lighting should keep the casual mood without compromising on providing evening guests well-lit paths.

There are several options when creating a casual lighting scheme. Depending on the mood you are after, you can have lighting align with the casual, country look, or have the lighting contrast by introducing ultra-modern blown-glass light shades, for example. If you want to put a spin on your casual cottage-style entry, you could retrofit a no-match, eclectic collection of antique fixtures and encircle the entry walls. If you need to add more light, install small recessed dimmers or tiny contemporary glass lights that encircle the foyer off a wire track.

Mixing light sources also reflects a casual style: Use lamps, sconces, and chandeliers to keep the light as well as the view interesting. Choose pieces that reflect a modern mode with minimal details and made of no more than two materials. For example, introduce contemporary lighting made of a material that is elsewhere in the entryway, like iron or brass.

Try something unusual that contrasts modern with casual country. For example, consider installing recessed lighting on dimmers in the entryway and edging the ceiling in thin strips of mirror, no more than an inch deep. For a finishing touch, introduce a wrought iron chandelier that uses candles in the

center of the space. Imagine how magical your entryway will look in the evening when the dimmers and candles provide a reflective glow.

If you want your lighting to suggest quintessential casual country, you might want to consider introducing a mix that may include some or all of the following: pounded tin hanging lamps, table lamps, or sconces;

Paul Revere tin lanterns; log and tin chandeliers; and glass lanterns with candles.

Consider, too, brass-based lamps and sconces. For brass table lamps, black shades work well, as do deep solids like terra-cotta, hunter green, or gold. In addition, mix in some real candle treatments whether they are sconces or a single, dramatic chandelier lit only on special occasions.

ABOVE When planning your lighting, make note of how much natural light you have. Here, natural light is maximized so that spot lighting is only needed for mood.

Choosing Foyer Wall Treatments

There are myriad choices to dress your entryway walls—from paint to wood to tile and beyond. Don't make the final decision until the furniture is arranged and the flooring is down because space constraints won't be evident until then. Once these elements are in place, stand back and study the room. Does the wall covering need to accentuate the style or can it sit back, quietly? Is everything so plain that introducing a print wallpaper is called for? Is there lots of natural light from a big window or is this a dark chunk of space that could use a variety of colors that glow?

Once these questions have been answered and practical needs have been determined, begin to explore the wall treatment possibilities that will enhance the casual theme.

Here are some design recipes to evaluate:

- Paint the walls with a contemporary, bright color, such as high-gloss or satin yellow, red, or blue.

- Paint the walls pure white to accentuate the brown and honey shades and shapes of the casual wood furnishings, colorful accessories, and collections.

- Bring in big color at the ceiling level if large pieces of furniture cover big chunks of wall. Paint the walls a very pale color to open up the room, and add a band of color, such as burnt orange or lemon yellow, that encircles the room. If the stripe doesn't appeal, try stenciling a simple design, such as a star. Or paint the ceiling a deep rich gold to contrast with the pale earth-toned walls.

- Consider creating a realistic photo scene out of tile—perhaps using photos of your children at the beach. Locate an artist who specializes in custom tiles—a person who could draw on tiles and then paint accordingly.

- Cover the walls with solid, bold-colored tiles that mimic the pattern of a country quilt or heirloom blanket or have a faux painter mimic tiles on one or a portion of a dark wall.

- Uphold the casual country mood with simple design statements; look at Shaker-style cane seat patterns and quilts for inspiration, and borrow one element for the walls.

- Lighten and brighten with a simple wallpaper with a light background and a well-spaced design.

OPPOSITE There is a lot to look at in this pretty entryway, including the view to the dining area and garden beyond. In this case, the simpler the furnishing and decorating, the better, so everything can be seen. Even the wallpaper can lean toward a quiet pattern and soft palette as it does here, while still defining the entry.

DECIDING ON A PALETTE OF CASUAL PAINT COLORS

The word casual suggests an obvious palette, doesn't it? Nature's palette of moss green, yellow green, gold, brown, and an array of pastels and richly saturated colors from flowers, fruits, insects, and birds all surface in fabrics, paint chips, and art.

Bringing the outside in and recreating the moods and light of Mother Nature is a favorite decorating technique all over the world.

However, choosing from such a vast array of colors can make decision making tedious. The aim of this section is to present some

possibilities and suggest color combinations, making choosing a color palette a little easier.

For starters, remember that a casual look can include either a light or warm palette or a combination of both. To decide if you want a warm palette, ask a paint store for

some oversized paint chips in a variety of colors and bring them into the space. Hold them next to the wood furnishings and any contrasting modern materials, whether they're metal or iron. Notice how the warm color chips embrace the wood tones and glow with them on one visual plane. The pastels, on the other hand, will act like a directional signal pointing to the wood tones, remaining on a distinctly separate plane.

Different paint manufacturers have different palettes so paint colors names aren't necessarily helpful. Instead, use the following color combinations as a base guide. Go to a paint store and collect all the brochures with chips, and it's immediately evident that names vary as well as color intensities. Put appealing colors together, and if possible, purchase pints of favorites. Paint trial combinations on poster board and place them in the entryway for a few days. Look at them in different light, and eventually you will determine a favorite combination.

In addition, investigate milk paint, a durable, all-natural paint made from curdled milk or cottage cheese, lime, and earth pigment. If you've scoured antique stores for furnishings, you know milk paint's unique country qualities. Milk paint works best on unfinished wood or wall board. Typical color choices include red, blue, white, gold, black, brown, green, salmon, mustard, and terra-cotta.

OPPOSITE When pulling a look together, don't forget that the front door can play a major role in strengthening the casual country mood. In this entryway, adding the pine table and terra-cotta floor tiles upholds the look perfectly. The cascading yellow fabric, pooling at the floor, keeps a warm glow here no matter what the weather. Notice, too, how engaging a simple palette can be.

ABOVE Take cues from architectural detailing for palettes and furnishing styles.

WARM PALETTES

The entire wall or walls of the entry don't have to be the same color. Try painting one wall a warm yellow, surrounded in white and trimmed with yellow. Another wall can uphold the palette with wallpaper. That way the yellow wall can serve as the background for an interesting piece of pottery or an old wrought iron mirror. The bright color will outline and emphasize the unique qualities of what fronts it.

YELLOW AND CREAM

BURNT ORANGE AND YELLOW

YELLOW, BURNT ORANGE, CREAM

ORANGE, CREAM, MOSS GREEN

YELLOW, RED, CREAM, MOSS GREEN

YELLOW, MOSS GREEN, TERRA-COTTA, CREAM

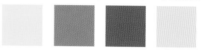

YELLOW, MOSS GREEN, RUST, CREAM

LIGHT PALETTES

Going with a light palette suggests a more modern casual look. To accomplish this, use any of the warm color combinations suggested opposite but go with their lightest versions as pastels or very faint hues.

In addition, integrate cooler colors in these combinations:

WHITE, MINT GREEN, SKY BLUE

WHITE, CREAM, SALMON

WHITE, YELLOW, CREAM

BUTTER, MINT GREEN, SKY BLUE, CREAM

BUTTER, MINT GREEN, SKY BLUE, SALMON, CREAM

ABOVE Keep the palette simple to make an entryway that's serene as well as welcoming. This pretty lime-green wall cover keeps this entryway crisp, clean, inviting, and stylishly country. Pale stenciling on the walls and bordering doorways adds subtle color. A quilt wall hanging grounds the table and greens beneath.

OPPOSITE The great thing about mixing modern with country is that attributes of each can stand on their own, and as a whole, they make for an interesting composition. Here, the open geometric copper stairway rail plays off the antique green of the chair below, as well as the round frame of the antique tapestry. The eye is led around the space and always lands on a new visual or a new color.

ABOVE Do not ignore the decorating magic that comes with using wallpaper. It can set the stage for a casual decor and offer an abundance of palettes and accenting fabrics. This entry is a perfect example of how wallpaper can be used to extend one room into another.

INCORPORATING PAINT TEXTURES

There are many ways to make paint take on new visual properties—such as sponging, combing, ragging, spattering, stippling, marbling, and wood graining. None of these techniques are difficult to learn, and each will add dimension and texture, while enhancing natural and incandescent light.

EXPLORING CASUAL—STYLE WALLPAPER

If you prefer the look of wallpaper, explore patterns that have country scenes to provide a pleasant backdrop for chosen entryway furnishings. In addition, look at some of the wonderful reproductions of antique wallpapers, or if your budget allows, investigate having a faux painter create a scene on the wall. For example, try extending the landscaping that's outside inside, so when the door swings open the view of fields or wildflower garden is continued.

Combining several elements is another way to add interest and a casual feeling. For example, sponge or comb one wall, and on another wall or two, install wallpaper. The fastest way to see all the choices is on the Internet—visit the Web sites of major wallpaper manufacturers to view pattern choices.

OPPOSITE An unusual antique door sets the stage for this charming country entryway. A simple color palette woven with floral patterns—including a needlepoint rug and fabric window shade—reminds guests of the garden-like setting of the home. Setting the floral arrangement atop a cement pedestal keeps the mood casual.

CREATING TEXTURE, DIMENSION, AND INTEREST WITH COLLECTIBLES

What else can be put in an entryway besides a table, desk, and lighting? How can texture and color be incorporated? Collectors, or those who want to start, may find the entryway is the perfect perch for casual-style collectibles. Here are some ideas that could be integrated into this area:

- Antique baskets: Line them up on the floor, atop a long, shallow table, up the main stairway, or on top of an entryway armoire.

- Hand-hooked rugs or quilts: Fill the wall, top to bottom, with five to ten in different sizes. These will add lots of color and interesting shapes.

- A collection of pottery, antique andirons, glass bottles, tin boxes, antique toys, old hat boxes, porcelain mugs, creamware jugs, or Nantucket baskets could sit nicely on a shelf or antique table.

- Use ledges of different sizes, shapes, and colors to display framed collectibles like botanical prints, maps, old store signs, needlework samples, framed antique linens, or antique serving trays with glass-pressed butterflies.

OPPOSITE Think about how lamp light with fabric shades can contribute to the mood as well as the entry palette.

ABOVE Here is an entry that, despite its balance and symmetry, remains interesting to look at from any angle. The key is in the mix—including art, sculpture, wood tones, and greenery. Create your own casual entryway by displaying an assortment of treasured pieces and styles.

DECORATING ENTRYWAYS WITH GREENS AND FLOWERS

No matter what style entryway décor you choose, adding green or flowering plants adds to the welcoming feeling of the space. Look for plants that are easy to grow and maintain, and consider plants that bloom continuously, like cyclamen and begonias, so you'll have color all year. If you have the space, consider topiaries, which can be the perfect addition of greenery.

As for containers, there are many possibilities. Consider containers a design accessory that will complement the palette and design of the area. If you're designing with a country theme, think about using unusual containers to pull the look together. For example, an antique child's sleigh could be the perfect platform for a row of colorful potted plants.

ABOVE In this entryway, the owner let the high ceilings and wonderful architectural detailing shine through by keeping the look clean and crisp. A casual mix of framed photos on both walls and a few interesting antique pieces add subtle color and texture.

OPPOSITE Sometimes the architecture of a home provides a ready-made entry mood. That is the case here, where a massive 30-foot (9.1m)-high wall of glass keeps the entry sunny and picturesque. Not a lot of design elements are needed to welcome visitors. A simple framed mirror that reflects the grand room beyond brings guests inside quickly.

RIGHT This country-style entry reflects the casual mood of this home and takes advantage of the season's flower bounty. An entry can be a calendar of sorts that always reflects the time of year in a special way. Who wouldn't feel welcome after opening the door here?

CHOOSING AND DESIGNING ENTRYWAY FLOORS

ABOVE AND BELOW Painting floors and adding whimsical designs adds not only color and smiles but dimension.

In an entryway design plan, a floor can play as large a role in the theme as desired. Today, options for flooring design are plentiful and run the gamut from ultramodern materials like rubber, metal, and custom-tinted concrete and vinyl to recycled barn wood and intricate floral inlays. With advances in flooring technology, color palettes are broader than ever and offer unique patterns and faux textures.

But where do you begin? Flooring is more than a look. It's a sound, a smell, a touch, a reflective surface. It contributes to the mood in the entry and can be a big part of what sets the stage for the rest of the home.

On the practical side, consider just how much upkeep the flooring you love will require. A soft wood floor, like pine, may be attractive, but will you love it when high heels put dings in it? Do you want a pristine, clean floor, or do you embrace what happens with natural aging and traffic? Think about that. Nothing is right or wrong; it's all about who you are and what you are trying to say about your home.

Before making a flooring choice for the entryway, consider how the space should feel, sound, and look. Should it be formal, informal, contemporary, eclectic, country, romantic? Do you want your shoes and the shoes of your guests to click across a hard, stone surface? Or do you like the sound of people walking across wood? It's quite different than the sharp click of tile or stone. Do you want to smell wax and wood when you come into your home? Can you imagine a polyurethane finish over new or refinished wood floors? Will the lasting smell be bothersome?

Finally, find examples of spaces you like, with design-specific components that create the mood, and write them down. Another handy tip is to keep a scrapbook of photos of flooring options you like as well as dislike. Go through magazines and surf the Internet, plugging in keywords like tile, stone, wood flooring, mosaic, glass tiles, recycled wood, and metal flooring.

LEFT To maintain a contemporary, clean look without sacrificing warmth, consider going au naturel with wood in the entry. Use the same wood on a staircase and on architectural detailing; the simplicity keeps the mood serene.

LEFT Create a rug with decorative glass tiles and give an entryway a versatile palette and unusual look.

CHAPTER 5

Formal
STYLE

LEFT This milky
white and brown
entry is understated
as well as formal.
Well-chosen, classic
furnishings sit quietly
centered at the door-
way, and the white
tile floor that moves
off to the left seems
to guide you into the
peacefulness beyond.

TO BUILD THE LOOK AND DEVELOP A FOUNDATION FOR FORMAL STYLE, DISSECT THE SPACE AND DETERMINE WHAT YOU HAVE TO WORK WITH, WHAT NEEDS FIXING, AND WHAT FURNISHINGS, IF ANY, SHOULD BE ELIMINATED.

Breaking the room into components is an important first step. Examine the actual entryway space: What is there room for in here? What is the focal point? Is it a beautiful window and view to the outside or is it the curving stairway to the second floor? Is it a long, narrow room or a space that's square or round? Is it big enough to spend time in or is it just a passageway? Focus on the good points and decide how those can be accentuated. For example, changing the shape of an entryway from narrow and confined to light and airy can be achieved with the right design elements.

Just as in any entry, natural light and lighting are important elements to consider. Whether the space is dark or over-lit can surface attractive design solutions.

Take note, too, of the architectural details of the area and see how those can be complemented by furnishings, wall coverings, or art. Closets and hardware also play an integral role. How many closets are there? Are the doors attractive? Sometimes these little details make a huge difference. If the doors look worn and tired, and the knobs are boring, they could set the mood in here, and you may end up treating the space the way it looks. In that case, consider refurbishing the doors and adding some new knobs. Investigate options on these details. You can buy new or reclaimed ones!

Take a look around and above you at the walls and ceilings in the entryway, and make note of the condition of these areas, as well as architectural attributes and shortcomings. Think about whether the walls will look better painted or wallpapered or whether new woodwork and detailing would add some punch. Perhaps a tired old wall partially covered in wood and then papered on the upper half would liven things up.

RIGHT With carefully arranged framed art on display, this entryway takes elements of formal style and adds a fresh, modern twist.

USING ENTRYWAYS TO ENHANCE COLLECTIONS

The entry could be the perfect place to formally showcase collections of any style. Use furnishings as perches, install ledges at different levels on the walls, or hang framed collectibles at different heights from wire that connects where the ceiling and wall meet. Wrap the wire in fabric to add interest, texture, and color.

Some small collectibles that would work in an entryway could include:

- Antique bells

- Antique needlepoint, linen, or decorative bead work

- Candelabras

- Clocks

- Doorstops

- Glass bud vases

- Miniature books

- Music boxes

- Pressed glass

- Shell art

- Wedding cake tops

- Sculpture

- Pottery

- Small paintings that share a theme

ESSENTIALS: WORLDLY
CONFIDENCE AND LIVING
IN BALANCE

FORMAL TREASURES:
FURNISHINGS INCLUDE
ANTIQUES, REPRODUCTIONS,
AND PERIOD PIECES AS
WELL AS CONTEMPORARY
FURNITURE, ART, AND LIGHTS

FORMAL DETAILS: WALL
COLORS SUCH AS MILK
WHITE, VANILLA, GOLD,
SILVER, BLACK, GRAY, SAND;
FABRIC WALL COVERINGS;
ACCESSORIES AND ART
SUCH AS GOLD-FRAMED
MIRRORS, GOLD AND SILVER
PICTURE FRAMES; VINTAGE
POSTERS AND TAPESTRY

Formal STYLE

Planning for storage shouldn't be overlooked. What is kept in the entryway area? Are the closets for guests only or are they a catch basin for family stuff from coats to holiday wrapping paper? Again, the way storage is used can influence design. Perhaps the best thing to do is to add shelves in that old, shallow closet, and use that for the family things. To embrace the formal look, consider, for example, purchasing a big, old antique armoire to house guests' coats. Now the focal point has been merged with practicality—perfect!

Flooring should be a primary concern when designing a formal space. How many times a day do family members move through the area? Does the floor take a beating from kids flying through the door as they drop sports equipment? Look at the existing flooring. Is it practical? Attractive? Boring? Sophisticated? Perhaps it's time to refinish the hardwood or paint it. Or maybe it's time to remodel entirely. You can accomplish a formal look that's also easy to clean and traffic-resiliant. Look at terracotta tile or reclaimed tile or marble that already has some personality through wear.

The final touch of a formal entryway is the furnishings. Make a list of likes and dislikes, and take a tour of your home to see what gems have been hiding in dark corners.

By the time these questions have been answered, you will have lots of good information that will help you plan your formal style makeover.

OPPOSITE The starkness of this formal black-and-white color scheme is softened by the curving shapes of chairs, wrought iron, and the banister.

FORMAL STYLE DO'S AND DON'TS:

Do see what's hiding around the house that might look great in the entry.

Do consider soft, subtle colors like milk, sand, and gray.

Do investigate fabric wall coverings.

Do consider antique frames that can be found at flea markets.

Do consider linen and silk for window treatments and chair and pillow covers.

Do visit historic mansions for ideas.

Do consider vintage posters for walls.

Don't forget about the role mirrors can play.

Don't get too busy with too much stuff.

Don't buy inexpensive rugs or photo frames—they will be noticed.

Don't ignore whimsical or unexpected additions for the entry.

Don't avoid mixing old and new.

Don't ignore the creative potential of ceilings.

DEFINING FORMALITY

Formality suggests a worldly confidence. It's not about matching and balance so much as it is creativity in balance. Anyone is capable of creating the look of formal style, even if he or she isn't worldly. Exposure to the elements is the key to developing the confidence that defines formal style.

When looking at the current shelter publications, you will see that confidence in home after home. Take note. Read. Examine palettes. Look at contemporary furniture, art, and lights. Keep a scrapbook of magazine pages that show rooms and things that are pleasing. Create separate sections for color, fabric patterns, lighting, flooring, accessories, art, and collections. Do this often enough, and the formal style of your entryway will be evident as you spin your personal design story.

THE ENCHANTMENT OF ENTRY CEILINGS

Do not ignore the great potential of an entryway or foyer ceiling:

- Paint it black and edge it in gold or silver to capture the elegant, formal look.

- Hire a faux painter to paint clouds, little scenes of angels, or multicolored butterflies swirling up and around the romantic entry. Or have a faux painter duplicate portraits or candids of family members and put them on the ceiling. Add a meaningful poem or copy a love letter on the ceiling. Give history and family a special place here.

- Consider creating a fabric tent in a dark, windowless entry. Gather the fabric in the center of the ceiling and let it cascade down to the floor or down to a natural mid-point in the wall, and button it with unusual tacks.

Types of Formal Style

When creating an entryway, scale back your wish list to the top ten items. Now focus on the essence of the entryway's message as the door swings open. Consider the following design presentations, and examine your list to see if you have the ingredients.

ELEGANT AND FORMAL SOPHISTICATION

The ingredients of elegant and formal do not imply stiff and unwelcoming. This style of entry will simply be fashioned with things you love to look at. If only things you care about are included, the welcome will come. Use the following elements of elegant and formal sophistication to help you think through the plan, not as hard and fast rules.

Wall colors of elegant and formal sophistication often include milk white, vanilla, gold, silver, black, gray, and sand. Choosing a palette like this provides a good base for all the rich color and fabrics that will likely share the same visual plane. Think about using silver or gold as accents on certain architectural details. For example, imagine vanilla or white walls with black window frames and sills. Now picture those sills with a little row of antique bud vases filled to the brim with roses. This example creates a wonderful view inside that leads the eye outside. When debating color for the entry walls, picture the entire scene.

Elegant and formal sophistication wall treatments don't end with paint, though. Wallpaper patterns, such as stripes, muted florals and scenes, and muted, tiny graphic patterns, will also work in an entryway. In addition, wallpaper fabric such as silk or grass cloth as well as seat covers, pillows, and curtains in fabrics such as silk or linen will add to the formal look.

LEFT You may not have an entryway with all this space, but you can still work with the space's assets. With a round entry, think about how to play off that roundness in an interesting way. No matter how low the ceiling, for example, a colorful scene can still be added. Here, notice that despite the fact that this is a large entry, it is quite simply furnished.

For elegant furnishings, try dark woods and period pieces. Think about creating a medley of pieces that functions together—a place to write quick notes or a place to showcase an unusual collectible. Accessories and art may include a collection of gold-framed mirrors—different sizes, different shapes, and different periods—on an open wall, antique portraits in oil (not necessarily your family), oil paintings of outdoor or indoor scenes, beach scenes, or farm animals in deep, rich palettes, antique glass vases, and table lamps with brass or marble bases.

CASUAL FORMALITY

In general, the most successful, sophisticated entryways keep things simple and convey one design message.

Wall color is often an important ingredient of casually formal style. To keep the country feeling and increase the formality volume, choose strong wall colors like deep melon, gold, burnt toast, or navy — colors that will provide a robust anchor for other design elements.

Wallpaper patterns can also provide a formal feel. Look into visuals that look like water-color paints, and consider patterns that suggest slices of life, like apple trees in bloom or scenes of country towns. Don't ignore the papers that mimic trompe l'oeil.

When choosing curtain fabrics, remember that linen is still an excellent choice for casual formality, whether the entryway needs a window shade or full-length curtain. Look at the window shades made of natural fibers—that buttoned-up, tailored look could be the perfect fit. To bring in the natural light and keep the view, consider simple bone-colored netting or real lace with classic, open patterns instead of busy ones.

For seat covers and pillow fabrics, explore cotton, needlepoint, and antique linens. If you find a needlepoint pillow, don't use more than two, and make each distinctly different from the other. If you find antique linens with hand-sewn designs, choose one linen and position it so it appears as special as it is. Don't mix it into a cluster.

When it comes to the accessories and art of casual formality, again, keep it simple. Find a theme that says just the right thing about you. For inspiration, go to some of the better antique shops or visit historic gardens and mansions. Study the details, craftsmanship, and styling of days gone by. Perhaps you will fall in love with a hand-carved umbrella stand or an unusual bench, and begin a search for one that will make your own special entryway statement. What will be the message that incoming guests receive? They will know that you love the past, and you want your guests to ponder craftsmanship and details that are often quickly passed by.

LEFT Here is a case where repetition is good. This entry features the interests of the owner—the sun and sea, in this case. Notice how the theme is carried through the mirrors and down to the floor level. Gold walls and a big gold pillow further emphasize sunshine and warmth. You could do the same with your interest, and accent accordingly.

WHIMSICAL FORMALITY

An entryway designed with whimsical formality in mind is all about surprises, smiles, warmth, and good taste. To achieve this look, mix together old pieces and new, bright colors as well as subdued, sleek fabrics and high-touch fabrics. One of the best examples I have seen recently was a magnificently shaped wooden cock-fighting chair that a chef fell in love with on one of her trips abroad. She adored the shape and brought it home and introduced it to her master bedroom suite. Draped with an unusual fabric throw and set quite purposefully off center in front of a glass wall with views to the woods and beyond, she made a big statement about herself and her love of art while making the observer pause and smile.

Whimsical formality is also about guts and confidence. You are confident enough to put things you love in an unexpected setting. Think about those pieces or styles you have loved but never bought—now think about it for the entryway. A big, 10-foot (3 m.) high mirror or fainting couch might just be your idea of whimsical formality. Or, how about an antique carousel horse?

RIGHT When there's limited space but you still want to make a formal design statement, follow the simplicity rule. Here, five components make up a tiny piece of real estate, but there's color, light, drama, and texture in the imaginative combo. Remember, bring in a few things, and try them in different places before putting nails into the wall. It's an evolution.

MODERN FORMALITY

A person who likes to concoct a recipe from taste as opposed to the recipe book may enjoy the look of modern formality. It's about pulling together a design scene with things that speak to the artist and collector in you. Adding a smidgen of real modern, such as a year 2000 designer creation like a red plastic chair or purple glass pedestal table, is even better to remain true blue to modern. The palette for walls for modern formality is contemporary and bright—from white on white to lilac walls and lollipop accents. Add modern sophistication ingredients until the recipe has all the color and shapes that say welcome to my home; this is me! For example, bring that black marble carved lion into the entry and sit it under a beloved glass table. Don't hesitate to hang an oversized modern art painting or antique poster over the whole ensemble. Just keep the number of elements to five or so and make, at the most, three distinct views. Mix unusual pieces, colors, and textures from the floor up.

LEFT Keep the formality calm, and conceal boring entry views with ultra contemporary simplicity. With the right carpenter, shelving with unusual twists and turns does not have to be expensive, especially if you paint it yourself. The same holds true with this false wall of red. Of course, any color could serve your design purposes.

OPPOSITE AND ABOVE Here the architecture
has the voice, and small art elements direct your eye
up, down, and around.

ABOVE Give small space its space! Here, an Asian theme with just a few decorative components keeps this entry clean and smart.

ROMANTIC FORMALITY

The entryway styled in romantic formality includes lots of texture, fullness, and soft colors and fabrics that seem to wrap guests in a soft glow. It's about the rounded shapes of European carved chairs and tables with lots of wonderful detail. Curves are also an integral part of romantic formality—curves on arm rests, backs, and frames. Straight, pointy, and clean lines are not in the mix. Pastel patterns, ribbons, candles, gold and silver picture frames, gilded mirrors, and lush fabrics that rustle or cascade are examples of the ingredients of romantic formality.

Romantic formality is about bringing collections together—from a row of milk glass vases to framed silk kimonos. This is a comfy place that invites people to linger, not just pass through. Merge old and new here, as well. To build the look, start with a favorite piece, whether it's great-grandmother's old, faded, floral needlepoint rug or a new baby grand piano that can be tucked into a big bay window. Once that focal point has been chosen, the rest will come easily.

OPPOSITE Count the design elements here, and you quickly see that it's not about high numbers but rather the stew of colors, textures, and shapes that make a look. The ornate gold frame and curving lines of the couch and table help to create this style of romantic formality.

MAKING A FORMAL STATEMENT WITH ENTRYWAY ARTWORK

Below are a number of possibilities to consider when choosing entryway artwork, depending on the statement you'd like to make and the available space. Think about developing a theme based on the area where you live, whether it's the city, country, by the sea, or in the mountains.

- Vintage posters, music sheets, and advertisements: These come in a number of sizes, shapes, and colors, and in a seemingly endless list of themes. Look at them as you would any art investment, and make sure they are framed professionally.

- Oil paintings, acrylics, pen-and-ink drawings, book plates, and watercolors: Consider using one massive painting so large that it can be leaned against the entry wall for drama. Or perhaps a collection of different media based on one visual theme, in a variety of frame treatments, would better suit your formal style.

- Photography is a wonderful choice to accent a formal look, whether you use black and white or color or both. Again, choose a single theme to create a dramatic effect, such as fifteen color and black-and-white scenes of winter in the country or twelve photos that each speak to a season and different terrain. Or, if you like to collect old photography, mix old photos in, too. Finally, antique portraits would make for a romantic entry. Imagine filling a wall, floor to ceiling, with portraits all matted the same in clean-lined black frames.

LEFT Always pay homage to your home's beautiful architectural detail by letting it come through in whatever room you design. Here, the floors, dentil work at ceiling height, and pretty doors should stand out, and with the proper furnishing choices, are complemented. That is the success of this entry's design. The collection of mirrors down one wall and the unusual pedestal between the doors adds warmth and interest. Think about the unusual collections that could complement your entry.

WALLPAPERING THE HALLWAY

Wallpaper provides a premade art canvas that can add color and warmth to your entry while enhancing the mood. But how do you decide what to use as you work at creating a unique look? How do you decide whether to use stripes or a floral pattern? And how do you choose your palette?

Before making any decisions, do your homework. Look through magazines and surf the Internet to see what the major manufacturers are offering in their various lines. Decide if you want a casual or formal style, a warm or cool palette, and how you will accomplish that.

If you want wallpaper to take the color lead, look at the furniture style and tone you plan to introduce to the area. Wallpaper can anchor the design components just as furniture can. If the entry rug is setting the palette for the space, look at that pattern and see how it can be complemented with wallpaper. If the rug is a large floral on a black background, look into a wallpaper that has a tiny repetitive pattern that picks up on the garden theme, like leaves. If you have a small space and the wallpaper you love will close in the area, consider wallpapering just one wall and painting the other three. And if you'd like to keep the foyer formal, investigate fabric wall coverings. To cozy up a big, cold entry, think about wallpapering the ceiling, too!

Look at the kinds of subtle things you can complement with wallpaper. For example, think about the big curve on the back of a bench you plan to put in the entry. Is that a detail that could be repeated in a geometric wallpaper pattern?

Don't be afraid to mix wallpaper, paint, and stenciling; it's all a matter of proper styling. And don't forget to look at wallpaper's complementary fabrics.

ABOVE Sophisticated patterns such as these can create an elegant mood in an entry, and you can build the look by following the palette or design.

LEFT Investigate mixing fabrics in the same design family. It adds another level of interest.

BELOW This wallpaper and fabric palette provides lots of decorating flexibility. The different patterns, subtle as they are, give the option of carrying the natural leaf theme and blue, yellow, or green colors to other areas—in art or pottery, for example.

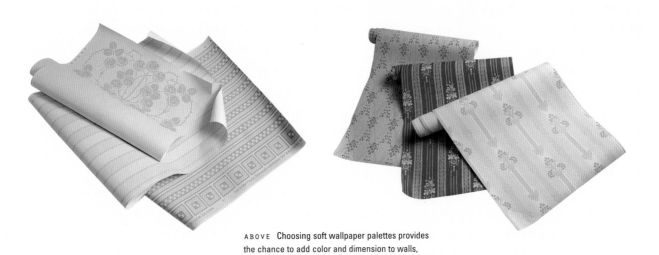

ABOVE Choosing soft wallpaper palettes provides the chance to add color and dimension to walls, while complementing warm or dark wood furnishings and accents. Unlike paint, wallpapers with subtle patterns create layers of room visuals.

CHAPTER 6

In Your Own
STYLE

LEFT Choose colors
that will emphasize
and showcase fur-
nishing choices. The
soft yellow walls in
this pretty entry allow
the chocolate brown
woods to stand out
and be noticed.

IF A SINGLE DESIGN STYLE, PERIOD, OR PALETTE SEEMS CONFINING AND BORING FOR YOUR ENTRYWAY, CONSIDER CREATING A UNIQUE, PERSONALIZED DESIGN RECIPE. THIS CHAPTER WILL EXPLORE HOW TO GO WITH THE FLOW AND TREAT AN ENTRYWAY AS A PERSONAL ART FORM. IMAGINE AN ENTRYWAY AS THE GATHERING PLACE FOR ITEMS COLLECTED FROM TRIPS ABROAD, SHOPPING SPREES, OR FLEA MARKETS.

An entryway can function as a three-dimensional photo album of your life and say something very special to guests, loved ones, and friends. The entryway's message can be clear: Here I am, come be with me in my home. Whether your collection numbers three or thirteen cherished items, a space or display that takes you and your guests to another place or time is very inviting.

For inspiration, make a list of the precious items you have collected and carried through the years. First, go through your home and see if there are items that you love, but that are misplaced or deserve a better showing. Next, go on an in-home hunt: go through closets, attics, or storage areas.

RIGHT If balance and symmetry are desired, go all the way and make a statement with several balanced elements. Do this for drama and to contain the unique qualities of the right pieces.

In Your Own STYLE

You may be pleasantly surprised at the number of things you have forgotten that might be perfect for the entryway. Separate the items into categories, such as photography, wall art, pottery, glass, family heirlooms, furniture, rugs, and lamps.

Next, on a piece of paper, rate each item; for example, four stars is an entryway must. The second step is to bring the larger pieces out to the space and position them. Once preliminary layout is complete, begin to fill in with smaller items. Try a few different layouts; take snapshots of them to see which one you like best. If you are debating three different wall colors, paint three 12" x 12" (30 cm x 30 cm) pieces of cardboard with each color and photograph each board behind a major piece in the scene to help you decide on a color. Try the same tactic with wallpaper samples.

IN YOUR OWN STYLE
DO'S AND DON'TS:

Do mix styles, periods, materials, and colors.

Do look for things that will help make a statement about you and your creativity.

Do look at gold-framed corkboards and ledges to help you display.

Do look at recycled wood panels, old marble mantels, and antique screens for their decorative qualities.

Do consider screens as a creative surface that can be decoupaged, painted, or covered in fabric.

Do consider antique garden accessories— from wrought iron gates to old stone pots— as possible additions to the entry.

Do keep an open mind about the artistic potential of the space.

Don't forget the display potential of high and low flat surfaces.

Don't arrange everything in a straight line unless it enhances the chosen objects.

Don't forget whimsy and humor!

Don't forget that windowsills can hold some colorful accents; use the natural light to your advantage.

OPPOSITE Mix textures in flooring, wallpaper, and furniture for an interesting entry view.

Creating Imaginative, Personalized Entryway Themes

If the design anchor for your entryway isn't immediately evident, peruse this section for inspiration. As you ponder the following themes, do not feel confined to just one theme; you will quickly see how you can merge two or even three themes together. Don't forget: Of all the rooms in the home, the entryway can be easily freshened periodically by moving things around, editing, and adding new objects.

TRAVEL TO NATIVE LANDS

Why not feature your favorite country in your entryway? It's the perfect way to merge travel memorabilia while making a statement about you. Go with a country theme, such as Africa, France, Italy, or Switzerland. Elements such as furnishings, rugs, and color can make your entryway beautiful and unusual. Isolating and integrating these styles isn't difficult if you understand a few basic concepts. You don't have to go back for a shopping spree, by the way. Remember: You can shop from home on the Internet in any country you wish!

ABOVE Take a theme of wings and angels, and bring it to the entry as this owner did. Cover walls with cherished things that say "this is me." Notice how the red brick floor mimics the hot sun of the desert view outside; the open door creates its own art framed in the entry.

To find the perfect palette to highlight your travel theme, look at the photos from your travels and note the colors in the countryside in native plants, fruits, and architecture. Look indoors for inspiration, too. Remember the colors, fabrics, and wall colors used in hotel lobbies, hotel rooms, and department stores. Perhaps you can't get that trip through the Tuscan countryside out of your head; consider hiring a painter to reproduce that scene on the entryway wall.

Every country has its own style of chairs, couches, and tables, so the furnishing possibilities for your entryway are numerous. The styles and wood used differ from country to country, so make note of the pieces that would make just the right statement for your entryway. Is it a French armoire or a handsomely carved Italian chair that, standing on its own, is a piece of sculpture?

Make a list of the treasures that you coveted in your explorations. Would a row of giant African pots enhance the entryway? Would a delicate inlaid side table like you saw in Rome be the perfect addition to your entryway, perhaps next to a window framed in a luxurious Italian fabric?

OPPOSITE There is often design harmony in discordance, and this is such an example. Here, antiques and odd pieces come together to break up a long, narrow entry. What matters is that each piece is here individually, not because they go together. Perhaps the owner has a story to share about how each item came into his or her life.

DOWN MEMORY LANE

Imagine turning your entryway into a statement that is totally personal and captures your family roots. Here are some design elements to consider when pondering a nostalgic theme:

• Create your family tree on the wall with photos, documents, framed letters, receipts, and handiwork. Frame everything in different styles and colors, using both antique and new frames. Or use just one style or color of frame for all the objects.

• Introduce other items at tabletop level —your grandmother's doily, the photo of the ship that brought your ancestors to America, or the wooden box your dad always kept his mail in would be nice touches.

• Bring a cherished, functional piece of furniture, such as a desk, stool, or cupboard, into the mix.

• You can create an entryway rich with family history. The photographs that line the walls can be expanded into a photo time line that begins with grandparents as children. It's so much more interesting than keeping pictures in albums that get opened only twice a year.

RIGHT Whether you are an equestrian or avid climber, use a theme to design your front or back entry to match what you store there. Here, riding gear hangs neatly on pegs, and a horse sculpture and painting add to the mood. It is understated, yet it makes the point perfectly about who lives here.

THE ART GALLERY

With enough space, the entryway can be the perfect spot to place art in the limelight. Should you choose this theme, discuss lighting with a professional to avoid under-lighting or overlighting the area. Also, if you purchase antique prints or photos, speak with a professional framer who can suggest special mat boards and glass that will protect art and antiques from fading. If space permits, think about getting a small, backless bench that can be tucked into a corner for those times you might want to sit and enjoy the little gallery.

What would a gallery be without paintings? One massive painting could be the focal point; give it a dramatic backdrop by painting the wall a solid color that sets off the painting's palette. Or, the walls of the entryway could contain an eclectic collection of prints, paintings (oils, watercolors, inks, or acrylics), and photos. Hang artwork at different heights; create clusters of topics or clusters of opposites to create interest, energy, and tension. Imagine hanging a 3' x 5' (1 m x 1.5 m) painting of a carousel and surrounding it with photos and pen-and-ink

drawings of the same subject. Some other art themes to explore include landscapes from around the world, portraits, circuses, illustrations of nature such as animals and plants, and images of the countryside, cities, buildings, and oceans.

Whether your pottery, glass, or dishes are the work of one artist, one style, or an eclectic mix, think about the interesting ways they can be displayed. For example, an antique recycled fireplace mantel or handmade wooden shelves could be hung at eye level. Think about making the shelves as a form of artwork by enlisting a craftsperson to create shelves using different woods and inlays. Make sure, though, that the shelves are movable. Perhaps different shades of wood with different types of inlays could mimic the patterns in your pottery. Or premade shelving in different lengths and styles could be staggered on your walls. This type of shelving would work perfectly for a dish collection; choose white to let the patterns and colors of the dishes stand out. Glass-fronted cupboards, trestle tables, or contemporary glass tables and shelves could also work nicely as bases for art.

LEFT With a monotone palette and an odd collection of pieces, as shown here, you can create a unique mood for your entryway. Hunt down the unusual by going to auctions and flea markets, and begin planning your entry. The simplicity of this space lets every element stand on its own, while a whole look is created.

NATURE AND THE SEASONS

If you live in Zurich and have been photographing winter for the past twenty years, you may have scenes of people, skiers, sledding children, piles of snow, and the streets at Christmastime. These photographs are materials that speak to the beauty of winter and can serve as the theme of your entryway. If you are not skilled in photography, photos can be purchased easily. Local artists may also offer paintings with your theme as the focus. Build the theme as deeply and thoroughly as you like. For example, include in your entryway objects such as framed front pages of newspapers that record above average snowfall; front pages with pictures of abundant spring blooms; old postcards with pictures of Zurich over the years; framed pressed flowers from the area; and local crafts that enhance the theme. Painting the floors a snowy white and accenting the area with a colorful rug with a woven mural of sledders or a Swiss skiing town may be another element of your Zurich theme. Finally, introduce an antique sled to serve as a pedestal for a row of potted plants.

The same design path could be used whether you live in Hawaii or Manhattan. Imagine designing an entryway with Manhattan memorabilia such as movie posters, a giant photo mural of the skyline, abstract paintings of Central Park, old street signs and maps, or framed restaurant menus. Add to that a three-foot high glass jar filled with theater tickets or wine corks, and you have captured your city experience and passion perfectly.

OPPOSITE If you wish to recreate a structure visited in your travels, take a photograph to an architect, and see how you can bring that experience home. Like poetry, decorating an entryway requires your own interpretations. This entryway combines Asian and African elements beautifully. Notice that not too many accessories are here—to avoid distraction. The small storage chest and wood figurines hold the wood palette.

ECLECTIC MIX

The key to creating an eclectic entryway is bringing incongruous things together in a way that is pleasing to the eye, while at the same time making the desired statement. Try visualizing these eclectic combinations —each is a unique art form with an element of surprise.

- A Shaker-style bench anchored by two, tall, glass cylinders filled with colorful marbles on the bottom and pussy willows poking out of the top. Behind the bench, a contemporary painting on canvas with big splashes of primary colors like red, yellow, and orange.

- A long, glass trestle-style table flanked by black sculptures. On one side, a lion is sitting up, on the other, a cobra is wound around a tree. On top of the glass table in a single row sit twenty-five tiny black-and-white African pots.

- A 5' x 6' (1.5 m x 1.8 m) canvas of a water lily leaning against the main wall with the floor in front painted to look like water. An Italian glass chandelier that is shaped like a flower petal or butterfly adds light.

- Four 4-foot- (1.2 m) long shelves, made of an evenly spaced mix of recycled barn wood and glass, on the main wall that faces the front door. On each shelf, in straight lines, rest collectibles of different heights and shapes based on a theme of pure white pottery. Or, instead of pottery, a collection of clear glass containers, old and new, filled to the brim with sea glass and shells, could enhance the entryway.

PAINTING ENTRYWAY WALLS

ABOVE AND OPPOSITE Use paint to brighten, lighten, expand, and even direct attention in entries, whether they are front doors, back doors, or mudrooms.

If you are thinking about painting your entryway walls a new color to create or accent a new look, try these tips for choosing and using paint.

- If the entry is a high-traffic area, use a satin finish so fingerprints and nicks can be wiped off easily.

- Paint color can make the mood with the same strength as wallpaper.

- Use light colors to open up the space; dark colors make the space cozier or dramatic.

- Learn about easy painting techniques, like sponging or combing, that can add dimension and personality to the space. Teach yourself by using a cardboard box that you've primed.

- Do not rush into choices, and do not ignore big, bright colors that can make a special statement.

- Ask the local paint store to order special large chips so you can see the color more easily. If that's not possible, purchase the smallest amount of paint of your top three choices. Prime, then paint a large piece of cardboard or gator board with the colors. Put each sample board in the entryway, and look at each during different times of day. Live with them for a week before choosing the final color.

- If you plan to hang lots of pictures or art on the walls, consider going with bright red, blue, or even yellow, instead of a neutral background, to let your art come forward in the room.

- Don't forget that painted floors can be eye-catching and provide casual or formal entry looks.

- Let your creative juices flow with paint. Be daring. Have fun. After all, if you make a mistake, it will probably only cost you a gallon of paint and a few hours to fix.

- Make one wall one color and the other two another. They can contrast or be versions of each other.

- Use pastels to create a soothing, peaceful entry.

- Remember that sometimes subtle changes in paint can bring a room together. So, for example, if you paint the walls of your entry the palest shade of lime green, have the paint store add 5 percent more color for window trim and 5 percent less color for other architectural details. You can push things forward or back depending on how much color you add. Experiment by drawing lines of color on a primed piece of board.

- Create a little board with lines of the paint shades you plan to use. Bring it to the fabric and wallpaper store. Or get a wooden paint stirrer and paint your palette across the bottom; that way you will also have a useful tool with you!

- With the right theme and a good faux painter, you can create a magical entryway —one that looks like a garden outside your door or one that mimics fabric.

CHAPTER 7

Mudrooms
AND BACK ENTRYWAYS

LEFT Here is a
good idea for a
backdoor entry:
an easy-to-wash,
no-scuff brick floor
and plenty of hooks
at kids' level for
coats and hats.

FRONT ENTRYWAYS AREN'T THE ONLY ENTRANCES TO OUR HOMES. MOST HOMES HAVE BACK DOORS FROM THE GARAGE OR BACKYARD, AND SOME LUCKIER HOMEOWNERS HAVE REAL MUDROOMS. THESE MUDROOMS AND BACK ENTRYWAYS ARE THE NONPUBLIC THRUWAYS FOR FAMILY MEMBERS AND PETS.

It's where we usually enter with groceries or exit with trash. For pet owners, it's the natural place to enter when returning from a walk. Just like main entries, these back entryways can become wonderful rooms—the difference is these rooms often serve more the practical purposes of storage and organization. That doesn't mean, however, that the assets, attributes, and design should be ignored in back entryways.

The purpose of this section is provide inspiration on what to do with this space and how to design and decorate it. After all, why should any room in the home be ignored—especially one that is used on a daily basis?

Analyze this space just as you analyzed the front entry. On any given day, walk in there and look at it. Is it a mess? What's causing the mess? The mess is probably caused by a lack of designated storage and organization. One of the first things to do is to make a list of all the things that need homes and think about how they can be accommodated.

Here are some storage suggestions to think about:

- Awkward, bulky items: From ice skates to hockey sticks to kites and beyond, awkward, oddly shaped items make storage a hassle. If you have a growing family, your home is probably overflowing with these items. Consider purchasing wicker bins or hampers for each child. Put their names on the front so they can drop everything in their own containers upon entry. If the wicker comes from a flea market, think about painting it a different color for each child. Consider wooden benches with storage underneath the seat, too. That way, kids can pull out their skates and sit there to put them on—without going back to the main part of the house at the risk of the hardwood floors!

- Small items: Shoes, school books, lunch boxes, sweatshirts, sports outfits, such as uniforms and running gear, and toys can multiply and clutter even the most spacious area. If there is space, build shelving, cubbies, and drawers into the walls—up, down, around, everywhere it can possibly fit. Distinguish each child's space by assigning him or her a particular color. If your children range in age and height, accommodate them by installing coat hooks at different heights. If they can't reach them, they won't use them.

LEFT Look at how a cheery palette makes this back entry come alive. Think carefully about the palette for spaces like this. The yellow walls and tastefully painted floors make this welcoming. And, with plenty of storage hooks wrapping the room, you're assured that neatness will prevail.

- Pet necessities: If you have pets, this is a great place to keep food, medicine, leashes, collars, and doggie bags. Wooden bins on the floor with the pet's name would work, or if floor space isn't available, use different wall pegs for supplies. Wooden ones are available; you can even paint their names on them, too. Then, store supplies in fabric bags on the pegs. A pretty pillow case with a string of ribbon or yarn through the hemmed area can make the perfect pouch.

- Gardening accessories: Think about all the gardening supplies you could store in here with the right containers. Some good gardening options in the mudroom include: a trestle table that can hold pots, seeds, and supplies; a steamer trunk; antique cupboard; or tacked wicker baskets.

ABOVE If you are contemplating building a back hall storage area, think about how to keep the look consistent by using the same wood for the walls and built-ins.

OPPOSITE Even the smallest little back hall can have a charming look and feel, as well as functionality. Look at how well this space is utilized.

Mudrooms AND BACK ENTRYWAYS

ABOVE AND OPPOSITE Make country furnishings
the theme of the mudroom but give them a purpose as
well. Here, a bench, table, and cupboard cater to the
gardener in the family.

Creative and Colorful Back Entryways

Don't be misled into thinking that a mudroom or back entryway should be conservative and serious. Instead, view it as a place to swing your creative wand, and go cheery and colorful. Use the following ingredients to create a rear entryway that incorporates both playfulness and functionality.

When choosing wall coverings for a rear entryway, choose happy colors, so that even on a gray, winter day or in the pouring rain, you get a color zap. Good choices for paint include red, yellow, bright blue, apple green, burnt orange, and gold. Consider a stucco finish if it's appropriate to the styling of your home. Definitely think about raising the fun factor by using different painting techniques like sponging or stenciling, adding a wallpaper border, or adding ledges a foot below the ceiling and wrapping the room in colorful pots filled with dried flowers. Tiled walls are another excellent choice; they're easy to clean and mixing solids with painted scenes will keep the area bright and pleasant. Or if that's too expensive, paint half the wall (or add bead board or pine paneling if that appeals) and tile the other half. Or cover the walls with photos of family members participating in outdoor events. If you summer by the shore, frame all those candids of days of sailing and picnics. Paint the frames different colors, and use different shapes and styles to create a happy room.

Choose easy-to-clean surfaces that can take traffic and abuse like stone, brick, slate, or one of the new acrylic, linoleumlike surfaces when choosing rear entryway flooring. Go for acrylics that can be cut into fun patterns or big color blocks. If constructing a new home, think about putting a drain in the middle of the room so you can literally hose it down!

If your budget allows, it's probably a good idea to have recessed lighting that points into storage bins, as well as a main light fixture that is centered in the room. Again, look at main lighting that will make you smile, like big paper globes.

Window treatments are the finishing touch in a mudroom or back entryway. Initially, it's probably a good idea to look at easy-to-clean, sturdy options like wooden shutters or wooden blinds. These treatments won't be affected by the elements and won't require washing every other day. Other good choices to investigate include natural fiber shades; these are rich-looking and require minimal care. You don't want to worry about the skates tossed over someone's shoulder slicing through a billowing curtain.

OPPOSITE Make a back door entry multitask. Here, it is a place to hang clothes, store sports equipment, dry flowers and herbs, and store baskets as well as tools. It's an earthy, no-fuss space that works.

Antoine Bootz, 47

Courtesy of Anna French Ltd.,
10; 107 (top left & right)

Courtesy of Ann Sacks, 85 (bottom)

Courtesy of Austin Patterson Disston/Durston Saylor,
6 (left); 7 (left); 35; 111

Courtesy of Austin Patterson Disston/Adrienne
dePolo, 7 (right); 132

Courtesy of The Glidden Company,
6 (right); 64; 65; 84; 126; 127

Courtesy of Mountain Lumber/Jeffrey Allen, 85 (top)

Michael Garland/Joe Ruggiero, Designer, 44

Michael Garland, 130

Tria Giovan, 17 (top); 117; 120; 134

Sam Gray/Bierly-Drake Design, 14

Steve Gross & Susan Daley, 21; 43; 116; 135

Mick Hales, 98

Rob Huntley/Lightstream, 106; 107 (bottom left & right)

The Interior Archive/Edna van der Wyck, 90

Jahreszeiten-Verlag/S. Gragnato, 31; 62

Jahreszeiten-Verlag/Bärbel Miebach, 94

Jahreszeiten-Verlag/J. Schaun, 70

Jahreszeiten-Verlag/G. Zimmermann, 58

Anna Kasabian, 20

Maura McEvoy, 78

Greg Premru, 25

Red Cover/Christopher Drake, 30; 83 (right)

Red Cover/Brian Harrison, 108; 124

Red Cover/Ken Hayden, 29

Red Cover/Winfried Heinze, 26

Red Cover/James Kerr, 40

Red Cover/Trevor Richards, 133

Red Cover/Andreas von Einsiedel, 114

Red Cover/Adrian Wilson, 28

Eric Roth/Peter Wheeler Design, 45

James R. Salomon, 23; 41; 61; 92; 104; 123; 128

Jeremy Samuelson, 9; 37; 38; 54; 69; 73; 76; 79; 82; 89

Stan Schnier, 34; 86

Tim Street-Porter/beateworks.com, 12; 24; 46; 74; 97; 103

Brian Vanden Brink, 18; 19; 42; 137

Brian Vanden Brink, Tom Catalano Architect, 71

Brian Vanden Brink, Scogin Elam & Bray, 100

Brian Vanden Brink, Jack Silvario Architect, 51

Brian Vanden Brink, John Martin Architect, 22

Brian Vanden Brink, Rob Whitten Architect, 49

Paul Warchol, 101

Tim Beddow/Elizabeth Whiting & Associates, 83 (left)

Michael Dunne/Elizabeth Whiting & Associates, 56

Brian Harrison/Elizabeth Whiting & Associates, 68

Rodney Hyett/Elizabeth Whiting & Associates, 16; 77; 102

Lu Jeffrey/Elizabeth Whiting & Associates, 52

Tom Leighton/Elizabeth Whiting & Associates, 81

Di Lewis/Elizabeth Whiting & Associates, 75

Spike Powell/Elizabeth Whiting & Associates,
17 (bottom); 32; 112

Dennis Stone/Elizabeth Whiting & Associates, 119

Andreas von Einsiedel/Elizabeth Whiting & Associates,
48; 80

INDEX

RESOURCES

Anna French
343 Kings Road
London SW3 5ES
England
0171-351-1126
www.annafrench.co.uk

Ann Sacks
8120 NE 33 Drive
Portland, OR 97211
503-281-7751
www.annsacks.com

Austin Patterson Disston
376 Pequot Avenue
Southport, CT 06490
203-255-4031
www.apdarchitects.com

The Glidden Company
925 Euclid Avenue
Cleveland, OH 44115
800-GLIDDEN
www.gliddenpaint.com

Mountain Lumber
P. O. Box 289
Ruckersville, VA 22968
800-445-2671
www.mountainlumber.com

First, thank you to Shawna Mullen, my editor. The books we do together are a joy in my life. Special thanks to Betsy Gammons and her great New York find, Wendy Missan—you surfaced spectacular entryways from 'round the world and made this a page-turner.

ABOUT THE Author

Anna Kasabian writes about interior design, garden crafts, home and garden preservation projects, and architecture. Her byline appears in *Yankee* magazine, *Coastal Living*, *Woman's Day*, *The Boston Globe*, *Boston Magazine*, *New England Travel & Life*, and *The Gardener's Companion*. She has also been featured on HGTV and public radio. Her books include *East Coast Rooms*, *Kids' Rooms*, *The New Home Color Book*, *Modern Nostalgia*, and *Cooking Spaces*.